STILL & BARREL

STILL & BARREL

CRAFT SPIRITS IN THE OLD NORTH STATE

JOHN FRANCIS TRUMP

JOHN F. BLAIR, PUBLISHER
Winston-Salem, North Carolina

JOHN F. BLAIR,

P U B L I S H E R

1406 Plaza Drive
Winston-Salem, North Carolina 27103
www.blairpub.com

Library of Congress Cataloging-in-Publication Data
Names: Trump, John Francis, 1963- author.
Title: Still and barrel : craft spirits in the Old North State / by John
    Francis Trump.
Description: Winston-Salem, North Carolina : John F. Blair Publisher, [2017]

| Includes index.
Identifiers: LCCN 2016058817 (print) | LCCN 2017002212 (ebook) | ISBN
    9780895876836 (pbk.) | ISBN 9780895876843 (e-book)
Subjects: LCSH: Microbreweries—North Carolina—Guidebooks. |
    Distilleries—North Carolina—Guidebooks. | North Carolina—Guidebooks
Classification: LCC TP573 .U5 T78 2017 (print) | LCC TP573 .U5 (ebook) | DDC

    663/.5009756—dc23
LC record available at https://lccn.loc.gov/2016058817

10 9 8 7 6 5 4 3 2 1

Design by Debra Long Hampton

Cover image: Wooden barrel © Kishivan/Shutterstock

Page ii, top image: Doc Porter's Craft Spirits in Charlotte, bottom image: Mother Earth Spirits in Kinston

Contents

Acknowledgments

Still & Barrel: Craft Spirits in the Old North State, from proposal to manuscript, came together during the spring and summer of 2016. From May through August, I visited distillers, toured their facilities, and tasted their products, which were all quite delicious. Many thanks to the owners, head distillers, and staff at North Carolina's craft distilleries, who were always welcoming and gracious, forthcoming and candid. They made this book possible, and this is for them.

My wife, Lisa Snedeker, served as my photographer, editor, and chief consultant. She was also head of encouragement and motivation. My twin boys, Jackson and Jacob, remained patient and understanding throughout the process, even as I interrupted their beach trips and mountain vacations with visits to distilleries. A big thanks goes to friend and neighbor Chad Roberts, who selflessly cared for our pets and allowed us to traverse the state over those frenzied few months.

Paul Jones of the North Carolina Department of Agriculture and Consumer Services played no small role in helping this idea become a book. He arranged visits to seven distilleries during one week in June. From Asheville to Kinston, Paul drove the state's busy highways and empty back roads. His photographs appear throughout this book. The state agriculture department is doing great work, and its partnership with distilleries, as well as wineries and breweries, is a testament to North Carolina's commitment to farms and farmers.

I want to thank my MFA family—my mentors and classmates—at Goucher College in Baltimore. I will never forget their compassion, guidance, and encouragement. I would also like to thank my employers, *Carolina Journal*, which falls under the umbrella of the John Locke Foundation, for their continued support and encouragement.

Maybe most important, I want to thank the staff at John F. Blair, Publisher, in Winston-Salem for taking a chance on me and for believing in this book.

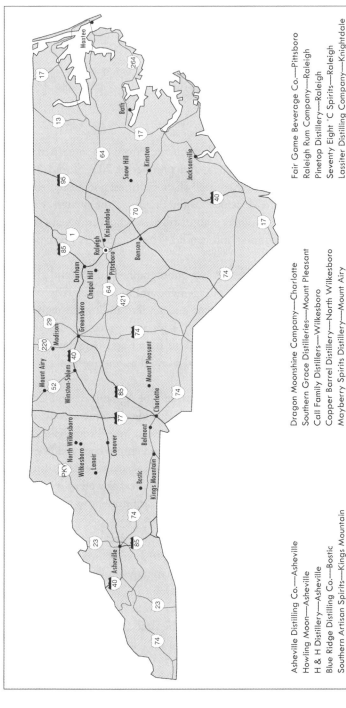

Asheville Distilling Co.—Asheville
Howling Moon—Asheville
H & H Distillery—Asheville
Blue Ridge Distilling Co.—Bostic
Southern Artisan Spirits—Kings Mountain
Carolina Distillery—Lenoir
Laws Distillery—Lenoir
Foothills Distillery—Conover
Muddy River Distillery—Belmont
Doc Porter's Craft Spirits—Charlotte
Great Wagon Road Distilling Company—Charlotte
Seven Jars Distillery—Charlotte

Dragon Moonshine Company—Charlotte
Southern Grace Distilleries—Mount Pleasant
Call Family Distillers—Wilkesboro
Copper Barrel Distillery—North Wilkesboro
Mayberry Spirits Distillery—Mount Airy
Broad Branch Distillery—Winston-Salem
Sutler's Spirit Co.—Winston-Salem
Piedmont Distillers, Inc.—Madison
Greensboro Distilling—Greensboro
Brothers Vilgalys Spirits—Durham
Durham Distillery—Durham
Top of the Hill Distillery—Chapel Hill

Fair Game Beverage Co.—Pittsboro
Raleigh Rum Company—Raleigh
Pinetop Distillery—Raleigh
Seventy Eight ° C Spirits—Raleigh
Lassiter Distilling Company—Knightdale
Broadslab Distillery—Benson
Covington Spirits—Snow Hill
Mother Earth Spirits—Kinston
Walton's Distillery—Jacksonville
Diablo Distilleries—Jacksonville
Scotts Point Distillery—Bath
Outer Banks Distilling—Manteo

Introduction

THIS BOOK STARTED WITH A FEW BLOGS that appeared on my own website, halfwaysouth.com, and were posted on *The Huffington Post.*

In 1999, eight members of the Kentucky Distillers' Association formed the Kentucky Bourbon Trail, an undertaking that juxtaposes the history at Woodford Reserve with the video-game-like Evan Williams Bourbon Experience. My love for whiskey and spirits intensified during and after a trip on the trail.

In late 2015, my wife, Lisa, came home and tossed me a thin brown and yellow booklet about seven and a half inches long and four inches wide. "PASSPORT" was written in all caps across the top. "You should check this out," she told me.

I did, starting with a call to Esteban McMahan of Top of the Hill Distillery (TOPO) in Chapel Hill. My blogs eventually morphed into this book, which is based on that original passport featuring twenty-five North Carolina distillers.

To understand where the fast-growing craft spirits movement is going, it helps to see where things began. Making liquor in North Carolina is nothing new, as anyone who knows a smidgeon about the state's history will tell you.

In the mid-1800s, lawmakers took a stand against wicked whiskey. In 1903, the growing influence of the Anti-Saloon League led to the passage of the Watts Act, which banned the production and sale of liquor outside incorporated towns, effectively outlawing rural distilleries. In 1905, the Ward Law extended Prohibition to incorporated towns of fewer than a thousand inhabitants, meaning that liquor sales were banned in sixty-eight of the ninety-eight counties in the state.

Though the Eighteenth Amendment, ratified in 1919, made producing, selling, transporting, and importing liquor a crime, North Carolina had jumped on the Prohibition wagon much sooner. A referendum vote on May 26, 1908, made it the first state in the South to ban alcohol. Even when nationwide Prohibition ended with the Twenty-first Amendment's passage in 1933, North Carolina did not ratify the amendment. It wasn't until 1937, when the Alcoholic Beverage Control (ABC) system was set up to sell alcohol in North Carolina counties, that Prohibition officially ended in the state. The state allowed breweries and wineries to operate shortly after Prohibition, but North Carolina lawmakers didn't lift the ban on making liquor until 1979.

"A hundred years ago, North Carolina had more distilleries than any state in the nation, and then all of a sudden it went away," says Keith Nordan of Carolina Distillery in Lenoir.

In 1938, the National Alcohol Beverage Control Association was founded to represent the state control systems, under which state governments took over the wholesale trade and conducted retail sales of heavier alcoholic beverages through its own stores. Today, North Carolina is one of seventeen states that employ this system.

The North Carolina Alcoholic Beverage Control Commission operates under the Department of Public Safety. Its overall objective is "to provide uniform control over the sale, purchase, transportation, manufacture, consumption and possession of alcoholic beverages in the state."

The commission set up North Carolina as a "local option" state, which means counties or municipalities can vote to allow the sale of alcohol in their jurisdictions. Today, county and municipal ABC boards operate about 420 retail ABC stores, which sell spirits. Beer and wine are available from any number of places, including supermarkets, convenience stores, breweries, and wineries in jurisdictions across the state that have voted in favor of it. But spirits — with the exception of limited sales at distilleries — are sold only through ABC stores.

As the craft distillery movement grows in North Carolina, the problem is that some of the state's liquor laws have roots in the 1930s and need reform.

The American Distilling Institute (ADI), which is "the oldest and largest organization of small-batch, independently-owned distillers in the United States," according to its website, was founded in 2003 with a mission "to promote and defend the art and enterprise of craft distilling." ADI now has more than a thousand members. Bill Owens, the founder and president, is a staunch advocate for craft distillers nationwide.

In Kentucky, a historically dry state, yet the reigning bourbon capital of the world, the passage of Senate Bill 11 in the spring of 2016 allowed distilleries to sell mixed drinks, which has opened the liquor economy even more. Owens says distillers in states with similar laws are selling 20 to 30 percent of their spirits in their own tasting rooms. "In the states that allow cocktails, the guys are making thirty thousand dollars a month at the bar. They're making big money."

North Carolina has some 170 breweries and more than 140 wineries. Brewers and vintners can host special events and offer off-site tastings and pours, unlike distillers. As Keith Nordan points out, alcohol is alcohol, whether you're having a twelve-ounce beer, a five-ounce glass of wine, or an ounce-and-a-half shot of liquor.

"I think they're starting to realize the benefit craft beer has had to the state," says Durham Distillery's Melissa Katrincic, referring to lawmakers and local decision makers. "Craft distilling, to have a similar footing, is going to need a bit more on the table. How can we get parity with wine and beer where we can pull our own special events permits? We're not allowed to. We just don't have the ability to be out in the community as much as the other guys do. We also have to figure out what we want as a group. What do we want to work toward? We're growing so rapidly, all trying to get our feet underneath our own businesses. As we get more organized, I think you'll see more from us."

Arguably the biggest boost for North Carolina liquor came in the form of House Bill 909, which Governor Pat McCrory signed into law in June 2015. When the "One-Bottle Law" became effective in October of that year, it was then legal for distillers to sell their products on-site. They can sell one bottle per customer per year.

"This was a big step for distilleries to be able to engage with consumers and sell directly to them the way that our wineries and breweries can," says Paul Jones, a media marketing specialist with the North Carolina Department of Agriculture and Consumer Services.

The law applies only to distillers making fewer than a hundred thousand gallons per year. The number of bottles a distiller can sell doing it one bottle at a time is contingent upon a variety of factors. Product and distillery location are especially key.

How Distilleries Get Their Product in ABC Stores

The way the current control system works, distilleries send their products to Raleigh, and from there the spirits are distributed to ABC stores around the state. It's up to the distillers to persuade the local boards to carry their brands.

Some products are widely available throughout North Carolina, as well as in other states and a developing overseas market. Starting locally is the general rule, but it's up to the individual distilleries—and, indirectly, consumers—to place their whiskey, rum, vodka, etc.

"Just because the ABC Commission in Raleigh approves my product doesn't mean all the boards are going to automatically carry it," Scot Sanborn of Sutler's Spirit Co. in Winston-Salem says. "Some may have heard of it. Some may have asked for it. I get invoices every night, via email, around eight, ten o'clock, and I can always see what boards are ordering. It's really great to see when a new board puts it on there. It means I don't have to call them up and say, 'Hey, look, I'd like to be on your shelf.'"

"It's kinda up to you to convince each board administrator to put you in their store," says Donald Walton of Walton's Distillery in Jacksonville. "And then, when you get in their store, which is a blessing and a curse, they have a North Carolina section. That's where you're going. I don't care if you're selling a vodka, a whiskey, a rum, that's where you go. So, when you're going into an ABC store as a customer, you go to the rum section and say, 'I want to try something different,' you're not going to see a North Carolina product way on the other side of the store, unless you just wanted to walk around and look at everything."

The system hinders creativity and invention, says Zackary Cranford, who founded Foothills Distillery in Conover. "You have to get your product listed, and you have to keep it in stores," he says. "It's not like a brewery. A brewery can make a one-off. It can make a mocha chocolate stout, and when they're done with that, they're done with that. For us, if we want to sell it, here or in [ABC stores], we've got to get it listed, so we have to make sure we have the supply behind the demand."

"It's become harder and harder for the current ABC structure to stock all North Carolina spirits," Esteban McMahan says. "The majority of [the ABC stores] don't. They'll pick and choose."

It's a struggle for shelf space. And North Carolina products, Donald Walton says, are the proverbial red-headed stepchild. Some ABC boards feature and promote North Carolina products, he says, but many others are ambivalent, preferring to focus on high-selling spirits such as Jack Daniel's and Crown Royal.

Some stores, such as the Madison ABC in Rockingham County near the Virginia line, highlight just a few North Carolina products—predominantly those bottled by Piedmont Distillers, because they're local and, well, they're big sellers. Piedmont was the state's first legal distillery since Prohibition and is the maker of Junior Johnson's Midnight Moon.

Oftentimes, even finding North Carolina spirits in a state ABC store is an ironic challenge.

Call Family Distillers has a display at the Madison store, but products such as Asheville-based Howling Moon are stashed among the mass-produced brands that populate the shelves. Recently, the Madison ABC had three jars of Howling Moon. But they'll be the last for the store because the product was "delisted" when it didn't sell enough units. Simply put, the store won't request more.

My wife asked the manager if she had tried Sanborn's Sutler's gin, which I found wedged among a gaggle of big-brand gins.

"Oh, I don't drink," she said rather emphatically.

I wanted to tell her she didn't know what she was missing, that drinking might actually help her do her job, but I let it slide.

I asked a clerk at an ABC store in nearby Summerfield if the store carried any North Carolina products in mini-bottles. He shook his head and pointed to the back of the store, to some shelves with a cluster of state products. "Everything we have from North Carolina is there," he said. On the way out, I noticed a pack of mini-bottles—vodka from Covington Spirits in Snow Hill—on a shelf near the door.

The North Carolina section at the ABC store in Oak Ridge is as far removed from the front door as possible—a literal rear corner.

"In general," Esteban McMahan says, "the farther you get away from your home base, excluding the big cities, the less the smaller boards are going to carry you. They just don't have the shelf space."

Joe Michalek, who founded Piedmont Distillers in Madison, says the practice of lumping together all state products and placing them on distant shelves ultimately hurts North Carolina spirits. "No one's going in and saying, 'I'm looking for a North Carolina product.' They go to the vodka section and walk the wall and say, 'Hmm, what's out there?'"

Store policies vary and, as the aforementioned examples show, are wildly inconsistent.

Product placement aside, Michalek calls his relationship with the ABC Commission "fantastic." "I've found them to be supportive and helpful, literally from day one." ABC boards, he says, are bombarded with an "explosion of spirits," and some liquor makers aren't asking the right questions or, conversely, giving the correct answers. "I've had nothing but positive experiences," says Michalek, who concedes the system must continue to evolve. "They're coming along slowly but surely. It's an old system, and it's moving along."

He uses Mecklenburg County, home to the state's largest city and a population approaching a million, as an example of how well the ABC system can work. "If you have a great, quality product and a proven proposition, you're in twenty-two stores overnight, you're shelved correctly, you're priced consistently. Go to another state and see what happens. It's a very different and very expensive world. It's hard to get in, but it's no harder than an open system."

Public-affairs director Agnes Stevens says the ABC Commission supports a healthy craft-distilling industry and works closely with other state agencies to help raise awareness of distillers and their products. "It is important to note that the 166 local ABC boards have the authority and the responsibility to select products that they believe will sell best in their communities," she says. "The local ABC boards across North Carolina promote products manufactured in the state with special signage and displays in the ABC stores that showcase the North Carolina products they carry. Customer preferences vary by market, of course. Not all boards are the same size, and not all markets have the same demands. The boards choose from among more than two thousand listed products in deciding which to offer for sale."

State-made spirits, she says, represent an "increasingly large number" of the listed items.

The Distillers Association of North Carolina

One development that has increased the visibility of the craft distillery movement in the state was the creation of the Distillers Association of North Carolina.

The distillers' group began with just a few members—basically a cooperative agreement spearheaded by people such as Keith Nordan and Esteban McMahan. Nordan helped Scot Sanborn get started, and distillers up and down the trail speak well of his efforts to jump-start the group, which centers on sharing ideas, answering questions, and eventually lobbying for changes in the state's stringent and time-worn liquor laws. TOPO's Scott Maitland currently serves as president of the distillers' association.

"We went from three members to five to eight to ten to thirty," Nordan says. "There were a lot of questions that came from a lot of people, and a lot of distillers spent a lot of money—anywhere from three or four million to a couple hundred thousand. The association has gotten a lot more organized.

There's actually some funding sitting there for lobbyists, advertisements. The North Carolina Department of Agriculture has been a great plus. Agriculture is the biggest business in the state, so we're proud to be associated with them."

"Rising waters lift all ships," says Melissa Katrincic, Durham Distillery's president and CEO, as well as vice president of the distillers' association. "North Carolina is not an easy state to be distilling in. So we're all trying to figure this out together, too, and move the industry forward. We're a work in progress."

"We're, like, 0.3 percent of alcohol sales in the state, and so it's not really us against each other," says Andrew Porter of Doc Porter's Craft Spirits in Charlotte.

The Locally Grown Movement

One goal of craft distillers is to persuade people to think locally, much in the way they now think about their food, emphasizing phrases and words such as *locally grown, locally sourced, non-GMO,* and *organic.*

According to Paul Jones, the state's Department of Agriculture and Consumer Services works with farmers, food producers, and food businesses to promote North Carolina products within the state and around the globe. "From our perspective, craft spirits are value-added agricultural products," Jones says.

The top industries in North Carolina—agriculture and agribusiness—contribute some $84 billion to the state's economy.

"The distillers that we work with use a variety of North Carolina products, such as apples, corn, wheat, rye, honey, and even sweet potatoes to create their spirits," Jones says. "In many cases, distillers are able to use ag products that are not suitable for fresh markets. This offers local farmers an avenue to sell products that would have otherwise gone to waste.

"It's our objective to make sure that working farmlands continue to exist, and I think distilleries fit nicely into that objective. Distilleries use agricultural products grown in North Carolina by local farmers."

The Craft Distillers Trail

In 2015, the Kentucky Bourbon Trail and the Kentucky Bourbon Trail Craft Tour set a new record with nearly nine hundred thousand people visiting eighteen distilleries.

In an attempt to duplicate the success of the Kentucky model, the Distillers Association of North Carolina, in partnership with the North Carolina Department of Agriculture and Consumer Services, developed the North Carolina Craft Distillery Trail. Distillers pay a nominal fee for inclusion.

A distillery passport—much like the booklet employed by the Kentucky Bourbon Trail—was designed to encourage people to visit North Carolina distilleries. The state supplied the first run of passports, which quickly disappeared from many participating distilleries. The passports were relatively expensive to produce and as a consequence fell by the proverbial wayside. A mobile app, "Visit NC Spirits," replaced the passports. That was replaced by a new app, "NC Spirits."

While I was talking to Keith Nordan, he grabbed an original passport, shaking it to make a point. "We had ten thousand of these, and they lasted about a month," he said.

Nordan handed me an early guide to North Carolina distilleries. It included fourteen distilleries and a handful of products, such as Cardinal Gin from Southern Artisan Spirits, located in Kings Mountain.

Most distillers in operation today realize that with growth comes a responsibility to stay true to their products and to work together for the good of the group, thus ensuring the trail continues to grow.

"A lot of these operations won't survive," Scot Sanborn says. "A lot of these have gotten their license, and nothing's happened. It's going to be interesting because I think the quality of spirits is going to have to rise as well. Before, everyone was putting out a moonshine. Some moonshine was good. Some was not so good. There are a lot of misleading, fake products out there."

The Future

Some eighty years after Prohibition ended in North Carolina, distilling has returned to the state with a vengeance. Distillers are determined to honor the past while capitalizing on trends and finding the perfect elixir to quell the public's thirsty demand for liquor in all its delicious forms.

Over the past few years, state and federal officials have rifled through a stack of requests for permits. They've approved products and sifted through label proposals.

Naïve liquor makers see legal distilling as the proverbial golden ticket, though it would behoove all newcomers to proceed with optimistic caution.

Scot Sanborn is realistic about this future and succinct in his analysis of it. "If I can saturate the state, I'll do okay, enough to pay the bills, maybe get some sushi once in a while. But I won't get rich off the state."

Conversely, the ABC helps simplify the complex processes of pricing and distribution. "We love the system because we have access to all the stores immediately," says Zackary Cranford. "It's not like we have to negotiate the price at all these different stores. They handle the distribution and all that, so from that standpoint it's fantastic for us."

Yet how many people will continue to pay top dollar for a bottle of liquor before tasting it? "You can experiment with wine, and it doesn't cost you a lot," says Troy Ball, who owns Asheville Distilling Co. with her husband, Charlie. "With beer, it's even easier, because it's cheap, compared to spirits. People aren't going to plop down thirty bucks or fifty bucks just on a fancy, just to taste what's in the bottle. The masses aren't going to drop down thirty bucks on a product they don't know.

"It will be interesting to see what happens five years from now," Ball says. "How many of these craft distilleries are around or still surviving? I think it's going to be really very, very hard for most craft people to survive outside of their immediate neighborhoods. Playing on the national stage puts you in direct competition with everybody, and with the big guys."

She says, "To be perfectly honest with you, all these people who have jumped into the North Carolina distilling industry have jumped into very deep water. It's very difficult to grow a brand in a state where you can't develop a serious tourism business. There are some distilleries who are lucky enough to be in very, very populated areas, and that helps."

A multitude of variables are at play, among them location and product. It helps to be in a place with hordes of tourists or in a metropolitan area such as Asheville, Raleigh, or Charlotte.

Outer Banks Distilling has built a following among locals and people who visit the pristine beaches year after year. People from Virginia, Maryland, Pennsylvania, Ohio, New Jersey, and New York. Repeat and loyal customers. "We just have such support from those areas," says Scott Smith. "The rest of North Carolina has been very good to us too, but we want to get out and be able to reach those people as well." Expansion has been the result of consistent demand. "We need the juice, if you know what I mean," says Smith.

Jeremy Norris of Broadslab Distillery in Benson began small and has grown slowly. Still, expecting a quick profit is a fool's errand. Patience and pragmatism will pay off eventually, especially if your products are exceptionally good, like

Broadslab's. "I have zero partners, I have zero investors," he says. "It's just me. That's good in a way, but it's bad in a way because stuff gets expensive. It's an expensive ordeal, especially when you start talking about putting up whiskey barrels. It gets really, really expensive."

His wife, Shelly, a certified public accountant, works full-time with Norris, which eases the burden when it comes to rules, regulations, and paperwork.

At the time Norris's liquor idea was percolating, the state had one distillery. At the time he started construction, there were two. Success was inevitable, right?

"I thought, *Wow, there ain't nobody in this end of the state. I'll be all by myself. It's kind of a unique-type venture.* Then another couple popped up. And in the four-year period that I was getting everything ready, I think I was number five.

"If you would have told me there would have been fifty distilleries in four years after that . . . One thing, I wouldn't have done it. It would have been too crowded of a market for me to spend the money and investment I've spent. But I'm in it to stay in it now. I'm in too far.

"We're serious about it. We ain't made any money yet, but we're four years into it. We're so far, we ain't turning back. We've got a lot of investment as far as farm equipment, grain, storage.

"Actually, everything's looking better now. At one time, I was, like, 'What in the hell have I done? I made the worst mistake of my life doing this.'

"This year, I think we're actually going to break even, or somewhere close. Maybe make a little bit of profit in four years. It's turned around really, really good, with the numbers and stuff. But to start with, I was, like, 'I can't keep this pace up. This is getting old.'"

The big distillers and spirits distributors dominate the industry and will continue to do so. Troy Ball considered setting up shop in Gatlinburg, Tennessee, which is practically a moonshine-themed fun park. The Parkway, the main road through town, is peppered with shops selling spirits flavored to taste like lemon, watermelon, peach, apple pie, and cinnamon. People tour the distilleries and stand at bars, where servers talk and pour without pause.

"Everybody's thinking they're going to get a level playing field, but there is no level playing field. It should be that people can come in and buy our products, just like they can in Kentucky," Ball says. "All these people who are getting into something they think they're going to make a fortune in are really going to have their eyes opened, because everything is so crowded now on the craft shelves. It's just crazy. It's a much tougher road than what most people think."

Yet craft distillers press forward because they believe their products pay homage to the distillers who once saturated North Carolina and because their spirits are better than those produced on a massive scale.

Grey Goose, a French-born premium vodka made of wheat and widely regarded as one of the world's best, sells fifty thousand cases each year in North Carolina, accounting for $10 million in sales, says Jimbo Eason, who represents Covington Spirits of tiny Snow Hill. "We're not ever going to be that luxury Grey Goose vodka," he says of Covington's sweet potato spirits. "The only thing we got on our side is this closer-to-the-farm, gluten-free, Putin-free, made-in-America unique product. What keeps me awake at night is, how do I have a business as big as Grey Goose? It's not easy, but I know it can be done."

North Carolina distillers are devoted to their craft, bound to authenticity and honesty. When things get busy, they simply work harder.

Troy Ball laments the faded legacy and the lost knowledge resulting from the Old North State's long dry spell. Distillers and drinkers alike must continue to learn, so "we can get people drinking mainstream industrial brands drinking actual North Carolina products," she says.

Bill Owens advises calm. Craft distillers will continue to emerge, and though some will fail, craft distilling will continue to prosper. "You look at the projections from the American Distilling Institute, of our growth, we're exactly parallel to the brewing industry, and we're at 2 percent now," Owens says. "We're wide open. People want authenticity, they want home-grown stuff."

He eschews talk of a saturated market. "I wouldn't worry about it," says Owens, who sees micro- or nano-distilleries—using stills of a hundred gallons or less—as the next wave of craft spirits.

"They want history, they want local," he says of customers. "They want to go buy that moonshine because they know it's from North Carolina. They want the real thing. Whenever I go someplace, I drink local. If I'm like that, a lot of other people are like that. The other ones who don't do it yet will do it."

Craft distilleries, like craft breweries, have helped to elevate the drinking culture. As consumers get smarter about what they're drinking, they become more discerning, more sophisticated.

"The market's a lot more mature now than it used to be," says Charlie Mauney of Southern Artisan Spirits. "When we first started, you'd go into a bar and try to explain to them that we actually make it. They were real close to telling us to get the hell out. They didn't even understand what we were talking about. But now, we go into a bar and try to sell them some liquor, a lot of times they already have it on the shelves. It's a good feeling."

The state is taking baby steps, but it's mostly headed in the right direction.

"Even as draconian as it is," says Pinetop Distillery's Jon Keener, "one bottle per customer per year, just being able to sell out of the distillery and really give somebody a reason to go on a tour of the distillery, really was a first step in making craft distilling actually competitive and giving us a chance to survive and do something different.

"We don't have the marketing money to compete with the big guys, nor do we have the kind of volume to make it worthwhile for every ABC store in the state to carry us. So the only way to really be competitive is to build up a really grassroots audience for your liquor.

"Just like the breweries, I think craft distilleries are the next economic development tool for different areas and different neighborhoods to really jump-start some progress, to bring in some dollars—which, in the end, is what the legislature's after anyway."

Keener hopes for the chance to serve mixed drinks featuring his spirits. Someday. "That's when people really fall in love with it. That's when you've got a good long-term customer. It will be revolutionary when we're actually allowed to make a cocktail in there and actually serve people the liquor the way they're used to drinking it. I think it's going to be a giant boon for the industry, and I think it's going to be a huge boon for sales."

And for North Carolina.

"Hopefully, the legislature will hear that."

I've had the chance to interview two legendary Kentucky distillers. Fred Noe is a seventh-generation master distiller for the whiskey giant Jim Beam. From a rocking chair on the back porch of the Knob Creek house in Clermont, Kentucky, Fred offered North Carolina distillers this small piece of advice: "Stick with your recipe, change little, and don't chase trends. Stay true." Master distiller Jimmy Russell, who has been with Wild Turkey for more than sixty years, offered this insight: "Do it right or don't do it at all."

To have a chance, craft distillers must be diligent, insanely dedicated, and willing to evolve and take on what some would consider maniacal financial risk. But more than all that, their products must transcend "really good." As I researched this book, I can honestly say all of the spirits I tasted were quite good. Some were exceptional. At the same time, all the distillers were winding their way through a regulatory labyrinth, simultaneously making liquor and doing what they could to keep making it.

Ollie Mulligan of Great Wagon Road Distilling Company in Charlotte likens the state's distillers to "a band of brothers," a moniker supported by a slurry of examples: the guys in Manteo helping Raleigh Rum Company; Rim Vilgalys helping Durham Distillery; Keith Nordan helping Scot Sanborn; Muddy River Distillery helping Doc Porter's Craft Spirits; Doc Porter's helping Greensboro Distilling; Jeremy Norris of Broadslab Distillery helping the guys in Manteo; and so on and so on.

But the once-small band is now an amalgamation of distillers with diverse thoughts and ideas—chemists, lawyers, real-estate brokers, engineers, builders, marketers, divers, and descendants of moonshiners on divergent paths but with a simple goal: making great spirits.

How This Guide Works

A search of the ABC Commission's website shows fifty-five North Carolina distillers with "active" or "pending-temporary" permits to distill spirits. The federal Alcohol and Tobacco Tax and Trade Bureau shows sixty-one distilled spirits producers and bottlers in the state.

This book does not feature every distiller that appears on these lists—some are still building distilleries, and some have yet to place a product on ABC shelves—but it does include an exhaustive representation of North Carolina distilleries from Asheville to Manteo to Jacksonville to Mount Airy to Charlotte.

I have done my best to profile all of the distilleries with products on the ABC's quarterly price list under the heading "North Carolina Specialty Products," which simply means their products appeared on ABC store shelves as of August 2016. This includes artisans who make whiskey, moonshine, gin, liqueur, brandy, vodka, and rum.

The ABC lists products from Tobacco Road Distillers in Clinton and Petzold Distilleries in Marshall, but neither returned my calls, emails, or social media messages, so they're not included among the profiles, which are based on interviews with the distillers and on tours of the distilleries. Also on the list are products from Gambill Creek Distillers and Tryon Backdoor Distillery, the latter of which has stopped producing liquor. Gambill Creek, according to owner Ed Gambill, was "on hiatus."

The distilleries in this book vary in scale and scope. Some, such as

TOPO and Asheville Distilling Co., have massive facilities compared with, for example, Diablo Distilleries and Howling Moon. Likewise, methods and equipment vary from distillery to distillery, yet they all make fine liquor. Many have won awards for their work. Speaking of which, when awards are mentioned in the book, it's typically in the context of a quote. Awards are subjective, according to judges' tastes, so I've made an effort—with a few exceptions—to avoid highlighting honors, medals, and the like.

I'm not a distiller, and though I explain the various methods of making spirits, this is neither a how-to guide nor a critique. Although most distilleries offer guided tours and tastings, the types of tours and the days and times vary. Some distillers offer free tours, while others charge, usually around ten dollars. It's best to call or check the website first.

What follows is a group of snapshots of distillers and distilleries. I tasted offerings from each distiller. I bought some bottles and was given some others, but all of the reporting and storytelling in this book is intended to be unbiased and objective.

I encourage readers to get in on the ground floor of an exciting and exploding industry by discovering what North Carolina distilleries have to offer.

And above all else, please drink responsibly.

A Distilling Primer

DISTILLATION IS A MEANS OF PURIFYING A LIQUID through a process of heating, creating vapors, and cooling, creating condensation. Distillation is truly a science, as well as an art. Methods and equipment vary among distillers, yet each gets basically the same results. Here's a primer.

Making Liquor

All spirits begin with grains, fruits, or starchy vegetables such as potatoes. The common denominator is sugar, which moonshiners often turned to—and still do—mostly because it's relatively cheap and readily available. Although some legal distillers still use a sugar base to make their liquor, the majority of today's whiskey distillers use corn—white or yellow—wheat, malted barley, and rye. To malt barley, the grains are soaked in water to germinate—beginning the process of turning starch into sugar—and then dried.

For rum, distillers use cane sugar or molasses. Distillers use fruit such as apples or grapes to make brandy. In the case of vodka, which is technically a grain-neutral spirit—more on that later—distillers can and do use all of the above. The grains are milled to a flour-like consistency —or fruits are juiced—and combined, creating a mash bill, which is basically a recipe.

Making the Mash and Wash

Distillers must have a good source of water, which, if necessary, can be purified using a process called reverse osmosis. Jeremy Norris of Broadslab Distillery gets clean, pure water from a fifty-foot well on his property. John Fragakis of Broad Branch Distillery keeps a large tank holding thousands of gallons of water from an artesian well in Surry County.

Distillers combine the grains or fruits with heated water to begin the process leading up to fermentation, which they get by adding yeast—a fungus, a living microbe that converts sugar into alcohol. Yeast has a big effect on flavor. It is so important to the process that some large distillers have developed and maintain their own proprietary strains.

Vann McCoy of Mayberry Spirits Distillery offers a wonderful description of how yeast works to make alcohol. "Your basic yeast biology: yeast eat sugar, they pee alcohol, they fart carbon dioxide. My job as yeast wrangler is to get my yeast to eat all the sugar they can to pee all they can, until they reach what we call their alcohol tolerance level."

This mixture, called mash, is cooled to about eighty degrees Fahrenheit. The yeast is added to the mash, which is placed in a fermenter, where enzymes aid the yeast in starting the process of turning sugar into alcohol. At this point, the alcohol content—or alcohol by volume (ABV)—will hover around 10 percent. The yeast works hard, creating a bubbling brew. When the mash ceases to bubble, it technically becomes a wash — or "distiller's beer" — and is ready for the still.

Distillers often carry over some mash from one batch to the next, much like a baker does with sourdough bread. In distilling, that's called a sour mash.

Distillation

The wash — or distiller's beer, or fermented mash —is pumped into the still, which is typically made of copper or sometimes stainless steel. Distillers can employ one or more of several types of stills. The most popular and common are copper pot stills, reflux or fractionating columns, and hybrid stills. The latter combine aspects of the pot and column. Many distillers use a variety of stills, depending on what they're making, and how much.

Distillers typically prefer copper stills because of how effectively the metal disperses and conducts heat and removes sulfur, which occurs naturally in distillation. The bad-tasting sulfur eventually becomes copper sulfate and clings to the still, apart from the distillate.

In a copper pot still, mash is heated to 173 degrees. The heat can come from a variety of sources, including electricity, natural gas, or steam. Old-time moonshiners, who heated their pots from the bottom using a flame, incessantly stirred the mash to prevent it from scorching, which would ruin the liquor. "You couldn't sell that," says Brian Call of Call Family Distillers.

The alcohol evaporates and transforms into a vapor, which rises to the top of the still—the cap—and is carried out through a thin pipe and into a thumper keg, or doubler—basically doubling the alcohol content—for a second distillation. The vapor then travels into a condenser, which cools the vapor—traditionally in a chamber containing a coiled pipe, or worm, filled with a constant flow of cool water—creating the liquid, which is high-proof ethanol. The liquid—how much depends on the size of the still—flows into a collection container.

A continuous-column still is just that, a tall multiple-plate column that pushes the alcohol content even higher. Think of a vertical tube fitted with small, round windows reminiscent of portholes on a ship. Each column, in effect, is fitted with perforated copper plates, representing a separate distillation. The mash goes in at the top and heads down meeting the heat, vaporizing and condensing, a process that repeats itself from one plate to the next. The effect is clean, pure ethanol of 190 proof or more. Repeated distillations effectively neutralize the flavor of the grains and starches, thus creating vodka.

Foreshots, Heads, and Tails

An art of distillation, says Top of the Hill Distillery's Esteban McMahan, is in separating the foreshots, the heads, the tails, and the hearts.

The foreshots—the first drops coming off the still—and the heads, which follow the foreshots, contain, for example, methanol and acetone, which are toxic. The hearts, as the name implies, are the good stuff. The tails, though they contain ethanol, also hold fusel oils and some undesirable congeners, or byproducts.

McMahan explains it. Distillers, he says, "concentrate heads to 1 percent of the batch, tails to the bottom 15 to 20 percent. That's the way I think about it. The methanol molecules turn to vapor at 172 Fahrenheit, the ethanol at 173. The methanol molecules are faster, but they're not that much faster. In a short column, it's like the first couple miles of a marathon. Anybody can win. Some of the slow guys manage to sprint for a while. With a tall column, it's like a full marathon. We're able to concentrate all those methanol molecules."

The progression from heads to hearts is abrupt. The heads are recycled and used as a disinfectant to clean office equipment. The tails are often tossed away but can also be re-distilled.

Distillers then gauge the distillate, or proof it down, to a desirable level. For example, an alcohol that's bottled at 80 proof would contain 40 percent ABV. Although there are other ways to check alcohol content—by shaking the jar and reading the bubbles, for instance—distillers rely on a hydrometer, which measures liquids' density.

The alcohol, once proofed, is technically ready for bottling, unless there's a next step. At this point, distillers can infuse the alcohol with fruit or spices or herbs and botanicals. They can add wood chips or place it in barrels to age.

Time in a Barrel

Deciphering myth from truth is best left to storytellers and historians. The history of barrels is unclear, but most accounts date their origins to the first millennium, or even a few centuries before. Barrels have since been used to transport everything from nails to sugar to gunpowder to fish.

Heaven Hill Distilleries produces a variety of bourbons and hosts tourists and whiskey aficionados at the Bourbon Heritage Center in Bardstown, Kentucky. Heaven Hill attributes the practice of storing whiskey in charred barrels to the late 1700s and a Baptist reverend, Elijah Craig, "the Father of Bourbon."

But the practice of charring the insides of barrels goes back much further than that. Identifying the origin of the first charred barrel is mostly a subjective exercise immersed in speculation.

Scot Sanborn of Sutler's Spirit Co. in Winston-Salem uses barrels that held four- to six-year-old bourbon to age his rum. He points to the bunghole—where the barrels are filled and emptied. People laugh about the word. Thing is, aging brings out flavors of vanilla and caramel, drawn from oils and sugars deep in the wood. The process of aging softens the whiskey and imparts a deep golden hue.

Bourbon distillers, for instance, use fifty-three-gallon barrels made from American white oak, which is both strong and porous. Temperature and humidity can affect the aging process, as air circulates around and through the barrels. The barrels, in turn, impart flavor and character from compounds within the oak. The liquid in the barrels also slowly evaporates, creating what distillers call "the angels' share," a nearly intoxicating aroma that fills warehouses and rickhouses from Scotland to Kentucky.

The insides of the barrels are toasted and charred on levels classified on a scale of one—a light char—to four—a heavy char. Whiskey distillers—and that includes Irish whiskey and Scotch and Canadian "whisky," too—have aged spirits for centuries. But aging spirits takes time, and many startup distillers don't have the option of giving up a couple of years for a barrel to work its magic. But those who do age their spirits will—in a year or two or three or four or whatever—eventually produce a better and more lucrative product.

Patience is key.

"That's the dilemma with barrel-aged products," says Robbie Delaney of Muddy River Distillery in Belmont. "In talking to all these other distilleries, you'll notice a pattern of how we talk about aging things. It's kinda like talking about religion, in my opinion, when it gets into this stuff. Everybody feels very strongly about the way they age their products. I wish we would have never dumped barrel one. Barrel aging is a crazy, expensive habit to form. But it's awesome."

Hyper-Aging

There are faster ways to age spirits. Hyper-aging, as it's called, means creating the depth, flavor, and appearance of a spirit aged for a number of years in a matter of months or even weeks.

This can happen in a number of ways. One is by using small barrels. The smaller the barrel, the greater the ratio of surface area to volume, so aging is faster. Other methods involve combining the alcohol with oak staves. Blue Ridge Distilling Co.'s Defiant uses oak spirals, which are dropped into large containers of whiskey. Foothills Distillery enhances and accelerates the aging process with honeycombed and toasted yellow birch staves suspended in the barrels, providing more nooks and crannies for the whiskey and imparting notes of butterscotch into the finished product.

Classifying Spirits

Most spirits produced in the United States and throughout the world must abide by esoteric rules and regulations to be called *bourbon, gin,* or *rum.*

The Alcohol and Tobacco Tax and Trade Bureau, or TTB, was established in 2003 under the Homeland Security Act for the purpose of, as its website says, "developing regulations, analyzing products, and ensuring tax and trade compliance with the Federal Alcohol Administration Act and the Internal Revenue Code." The TTB controls things such as labeling, advertising, production, and importation. It also classifies spirits.

For a complete and detailed list of rules, categories, and classifications, visit ttb.gov.

Spirits Produced in North Carolina Distilleries

Brandy: Brandy is made using fruits such as crushed grapes or, in regard to Carolina Distillery in Lenoir, pure apple juice. It's typically aged in oak barrels and is bottled at a much higher proof than wine, for example.

Gin: Gin is distilled in a manner similar to vodka, but it's infused with herbs and botanicals, predominately juniper berries. Recipes vary widely, as distillers infuse their gins with things such as orange and grapefruit peel, orris root, and cardamom. Some distillers use as many as a dozen or more botanicals.

There are several styles of gin, including London dry, the style for most major brands, and navy strength, which also can apply to rum. To earn the military moniker, navy-strength gins must be 57 percent alcohol, a nineteenth-century rule from the British navy, because, if spilled, the story goes, the high-proof gin wouldn't ruin gunpowder. While typically a product in the United Kingdom, navy-strength gin is an emerging spirit in the United States.

Liqueur: This sweet alcoholic beverage, frequently taken with dessert, often starts with neutral-grain spirits. Examples from North Carolina distillers include Krupnikas, a honey liqueur from Brothers Vilgalys Spirits, and the lemon-favored Limoncello from Seventy Eight °C Spirits.

Moonshine: Moonshine, which gets its name because illegal distillers produced it by the light of the moon, isn't classified as a spirit, which means it isn't defined by a set of rules, as are bourbon, scotch, and most other spirits. It's typically made from corn—thus the moniker "corn liquor." It's also been called "white lightning" and "rotgut."

Rum: To be called rum, a spirit must be made from sugarcane or molasses. Distillers often age it in oak barrels, giving it a golden color and a complex character. Distillers also infuse spices such as cloves and cinnamon, which give it a warm, earthy flavor. Outer Banks Distilling offers a delicious Kill Devil Rum, made with pecans and honey.

Vodka: Technically, vodka is a grain-neutral spirit, or pure ethanol—about 190 proof. Water is added to proof the spirit to a drinkable level. Grain-neutral spirits are mostly odorless and tasteless because any flavor from the source—grain, fruit, or starch, including potatoes and sweet potatoes—has been stripped away. However, some distillers such as Covington Spirits, which makes a sweet potato vodka, are careful to keep some flavor from the source. Distillers often add flavors such as citrus, other fruits, and peppers.

Whiskey: This is the broadest and most complicated of liquor categories. To be called *whiskey*, the spirit must start with a grain such as corn, barley, or rye. Some distillers use wheat to mellow the flavors. Whiskey is typically aged in American white oak barrels or hyper-aged using chips, staves, or, for Blue Ridge's Defiant, oak spirals. Whiskey falls into many classifications, depending on where it was made and with what ingredients and mash bill. For example, Great Wagon Road Distilling Company and Blue Ridge Distilling Co. make their whiskeys using 100 percent barley malt, which is similar to scotch. To be called a *rye whiskey*, the distillate must contain at least 51 percent rye. To be called *bourbon*, it must be 51 percent corn, must be aged in a new charred American white oak barrel, and must be made in the United States. It must be distilled no higher than 160 proof and barreled at no more than 125 proof. To be called *corn whiskey*, the mash must contain at least 80 percent corn and must be distilled to no more than 160 proof. By the way, in Scotland and Canada, it's spelled *whisky*. In the United States and Ireland, it's *whiskey*. This book goes with *whiskey* unless the distiller brands it otherwise.

Grain-Neutral Spirits: By definition, grain-neutral spirits are ethanol, continuously distilled to reach about 190 proof. Alcohol producers often re-distill or transform the spirits, making gin or other flavored spirits.

Asheville Distilling Co.

12 Old Charlotte Highway, Suite T
Asheville, NC 28803
ashevilledistilling.com
828-575-2000
The distillery offers tours and tastings at 5
and 6 P.M. Friday and Saturday.

INTRODUCING TROY BALL, maker of Troy & Sons whiskeys, to liquor connoisseurs is not unlike presenting Joe Montana to a cadre of seasoned sportswriters. Even if they haven't met, they are certainly quite familiar with him.

Ball has appeared on the Discovery Channel's *Moonshiners* and has been featured in a slew of TV news segments, short documentaries, and magazine articles. *Southern Living* named her distillery, Asheville Distilling Co., among the best in the South, alongside stalwarts such as Jim Beam and Buffalo Trace and North Carolina counterpart Top of the Hill.

It's recognition that's well deserved and well earned. Hard earned.

"This is the Troy story," says her husband, Charlie Ball, also a big part of the distillery. "She's the founder. We're kind of background guys."

The Balls came to North Carolina from Texas more than a dozen years ago. Their first official distillation was in 2010. "I actually went and started learning to make moonshine with illegal moonshine makers," Troy says. "The first batch I did was in 2008."

Troy & Sons whiskeys—the 80-proof Platinum, the Blonde, and the Oak Reserve—are now available in fourteen states. Made from North Carolina corn and wheat and produced in a German-made Kothe still, they are testaments to ingenuity and perseverance.

But it's much more complicated than that. Arduous and difficult, surely. Heart rending? That, too.

"How much shit can you have thrown at you in life?" asks Charlie Ball. "We had two special-needs kids who weren't expected to live to be ten, and they'll turn thirty and twenty-eight this year."

Troy Ball is a successful businesswoman, an author, and an advocate for children with special needs. She also makes some darn fine whiskey.

"I was interested in finding a business that I could create," she says. "I was in a place in my life that I had a little more time than I had previously. My boys were healthier than they had ever been. I met the old men in Madison County and that area, and they were bringing us moonshine."

Some wasn't so good. Some, though, was quite good. Of course, the 'shiners kept most of that for themselves.

"I thought, *My gosh, I wonder if this product's on the market*," Troy says. "At that time, there were only about three white, sorta moonshine products available, and none of them were well made, like these old men could make. I just got to thinking, *Why aren't we drinking American cocktails instead of Russian vodka cocktails?* It just seemed like the hole in the doughnut—what was missing in the marketplace. It was also very authentic, an American story. And I thought that was something that should appeal to people. That's why I got into the business."

When one of their children was quite ill, the Balls ate in a restaurant across the street from the hospital for about six consecutive weeks. "They served Crooked Creek corn grits, which we had most mornings," says Charlie.

One day, in walked John McEntire. He was delivering grits. His grits. Troy also met McEntire, along with Oscar Wong, the founder of Highland Brewing Company in Asheville. "That's how it came together," Charlie says.

"It was fun in the beginning, because it was just me and John McEntire, who was helping me," Troy says. "He let me get a permit on his family farm, and he was an industrious former science teacher, low-key and jovial. So whatever crazy ideas I came up with, he would jump right in and help get the problem solved. He had been around some moonshine making, but he had never really made moonshine himself. We were learning together, and those were some of the best days, that year and a half or so that we spent there in Old Fort just experimenting with formulas and recipes and different grain mixtures and different milling techniques and different filtration techniques. All of that."

Old Fort is in neighboring McDowell County. Fewer than a thousand people live in the town, best known for its thirty-foot granite arrowhead and historic train depot—painted bright orange—near its center. According to visitnc.com, the arrowhead was dedicated in 1930 to honor the peace between pioneers and Native Americans. Some six thousand people looked on as Cherokee and Catawba chiefs smoked "a pipe of peace for the first time in history," according to one account.

Asheville Distilling Co., which produces Troy & Sons whiskeys, occupies an inviting space in Asheville that it shares with Highland Brewing Company.

Photo by North Carolina Department of Agriculture and Consumer Services (NCDA&CS)

Old Fort is near the Crooked Creek community, where McEntire grows heirloom corn and red turkey wheat for the Balls' whiskey. His farm has been in the family for generations. When the corn was tested in a lab at the University of Tennessee, researchers were startled by its fat content, which was the highest they had seen. They tested it more than once, with the same result.

But as the saying goes, fat means flavor. "Modern grains have evolved to be leaner," Charlie says. "Heirloom grains have more flavor, more character, more taste, more aroma. They're hard to grow. This is a single ear of corn on a stalk." The cornstalks grow as high as fifteen feet, which translates into low yields.

"We tried to grow it in the Piedmont, we tried to grow it in Texas, we tried to grow it in Illinois," Charlie says. "It failed in all locations. It's a mountain corn. It's like us—it does not like hot August nights."

Troy & Sons calls its white heirloom spirit "moonshine," but it's really whiskey, made with 100 percent Crooked Creek corn. "It's high quality, it's consistent, it's got flavor, character, aroma, and taste that vodka doesn't have," Charlie says. "The Platinum is a fairly unique profile. It's got some notes you wouldn't find in a commodity grain. This is a hard way to run a business. Grow the grain, ferment the grain, distill the grain. We're plow-to-pour."

The distillery's Blonde has white corn but also includes McEntire's turkey red wheat, another heirloom grain, which Russian Mennonites fleeing the czar brought to the United States in the 1880s.

"We distill and barrel separately, and then we blend, and we blend like we want to blend," Charlie says. "Every barrel's different and every harvest is different, so we basically blend it to taste. It might be 20 percent, it might be 40 percent wheat. It's going to vary. We'll start about 30, and we'll decide if we want more wheat or less wheat."

Charlie says corn and wheat are the smoothest of grains, that rye is the "brat" of grains, and that barley can be bitter. "We're engineering out the burn and the bite. We're making super smooth whiskey. We make what we like. All of our whiskeys have an heirloom grain in them. Because Troy is the DNA of the brand, it's got to be smooth. If it's not smooth, it doesn't have her name on it. Smooth to a fault. We can't compete with the burn-and-bite guys in a competition."

Friends and neighbors gave the Balls a lot of moonshine. Much of it was free of odor and flavor, made mostly with sugar. It wasn't good.

"The story we think is true, because we've heard it a thousand times around here, is, pre-Prohibition, they only had grain. They didn't have sugar in a bag," Charlie says. "During Prohibition, you could smell cooking mash a mile away. But you can't smell fermenting sugar because it has no aroma. So they switched to sugar during Prohibition," resulting in "an entire generation and a half of people who didn't know how to make whiskey from grain."

The Balls had other ideas. They wanted a kinder, softer spirit—a whiskey Troy now calls the best in America. No hearts and no tails. So Charlie built her a five-gallon pressure cooker. Then came a thumper keg and a direct-fire still.

It was primitive, he says. "I'd go out and help design something, build something, and I'm shaking my head, thinking, *How are you ever going to make any money doing this?* It wasn't until I realized that she was on to something—that making a drinkable moonshine that tasted good had a marketplace. We built the original small test facility on John's farm, which is still there. Troy wouldn't quit trying to figure it out, so I said, 'Look, if we're going to do it, let's go talk to Oscar. He knows something about making stuff.'"

Don't incrementalize, advised Oscar Wong, who owns the massive building in East Asheville that the brewer and distillers now share. He told the Balls to buy the biggest and best still they could afford.

In 2010, they ordered a two-thousand-liter German-made Kothe still, which they received almost nine months later. Things soon got, well, busy. The local press came, followed by magazines and networks, including CBS and NBC.

"We were shipping a pallet a day, working all night," Charlie says. "We knew we weren't going to be able to catch up. I ordered another still. I said, 'Guys, I want it three times the size of the one we have.'"

Can't do it. Sorry, the still makers told him, directly and without equivocation.

"I said, 'I'm coming to Germany, and we're going to figure it out.' We ended up being two and a half times bigger because we couldn't get a three-X-size still in the container, and I wasn't willing to ship it open-deck. It's just too risky. You put it in a crate and you sit on top of the ship, and something happens to it, you're screwed."

Charlie defines—in terms characteristic of speed and precision—the three principal makers of German stills. "CARL's kind of the Mercedes, Holstein is kind of the BMW, and this"—the Kothe still—"is the Porsche. This is the one that's the hardest to run, and it comes with no manual. This is the one that's not for the faint of heart. You get no spare parts. You have to install it yourself. It's all in German, and you're all on your own. This took some engineering. We didn't have a consultant. We just figured it out."

The Balls place their smooth Blonde whiskey in patented honeycomb barrels, the exposed grain effectively increasing the surface area and, in turn, advancing absorption and aging. "If you want to age quickly, buy high-quality wood, expose it to a lot of surface area, and put it in a hot room." The room Charlie refers to is virtually a small rickhouse, the top row heated to as high as 138 degrees, which effectively provides a week of age for each day of storage.

"Desperation breeds inspiration," he says. "You want to have good-quality whiskey early, you can buy five-gallon baby barrels and go broke. We did a few fifteen-gallon test barrels, just to see, but we quickly went to fifty-threes, because we knew we'd never be able to make enough. We've got twenty thousand cases of fully aged whiskey sitting ready to bottle. We've probably got the biggest inventory for North Carolina."

The Oak Reserve is aged in used bourbon barrels from the Woodford Reserve distillery in Versailles, Kentucky. Wood chips are added, says Charlie, to brighten it a bit. "It's our version of scotch without the dirt. There's no peat." It's the distillery's second-best seller, behind the moonshine. "Scotch without the dirt and bourbon without the bite," he says.

Troy & Sons also makes flavored whiskeys—a nectarine and a cinnamon. Its distribution is limited to North Carolina and Florida.

"We believe in objectivity," Charlie says. "This is science. People think it's art. It's science. Essentially, everything about this is science. If you treat it that way, and you objectify it, and you figure out what people like, that's what you ought to make."

As the operator of one of the state's first distilleries since Prohibition, Troy Ball has played no small role in helping craft legislation to eradicate what she sees as obsolete rules involving spirits. "The more people who come to the distillery and buy the whiskey and take it home to their states, the more the brands get known. It's just a fact," she says. "We're going to make something we like, because we're selfish. But it's easier to sell something you love. It's hard to sell something you don't."

The original passport for the North Carolina Craft Distillery Trail
Photo by NCDA&CS

Crooked Creek

Troy Ball of Asheville Distilling Co. was determined to make good whiskey, and she decided she wanted to make it with white corn. She found John McEntire, whose Peaceful Valley Farm and mill near Old Fort is less than a half-hour east of the distillery. She ordered a hundred pounds.

She arrived "in a little white Mercedes. I had it bagged up and ready for her," says McEntire. He speaks slowly, each word significant, purposeful. "I loaded it in the back of her car, and curiosity got the best of me. I said, 'What on earth do you want with that corn?' She told me, and it was funny to me, because that didn't add up. But I said, 'I'll tell you what. We might do a little trading now.'"

Corn for moonshine.

"To make a long story short, I helped them get started, up here on the farm."

For the better part of two years, they tested corn. Variety after variety. "We started out, believe it or not, in a five-gallon pressure pot." He laughs and shakes his head, which is covered with a bush hat. It's midafternoon, and the temperature has long since exceeded ninety degrees. He's barely sweating.

"We had lots of good times."

McEntire and Ball compared and contrasted. Nothing was better than McEntire's heirloom Crooked Creek white corn, which was commonplace on the farm as far back as sixty years ago. "People used it as their bread corn, and all the moonshiners loved it for the moonshine," McEntire says. "But it's good corn. We kept it going in my family. It was just about died out, but my dad and my granddad both liked cornbread, and we grew a little and saved the seed. I decided to start grinding some on an old stone mill. One thing led to another, and I started making grits and selling a few."

The Sierra Nevada brewery in Mills River, he says, buys two hundred pounds of grits at a time for its restaurant. Crooked Creek grits

Turkey red wheat on McEntire's farm. The Balls use the heirloom wheat in their smooth Blonde whiskey.
Photo by NCDA&CS

are available at the Balls' distillery. The corn, to some people, is at its best in their whiskey.

McEntire's family has farmed its land in the Crooked Creek community near Old Fort since the mid-1880s, his grandfather carving out a piece of land and spending the last fifteen or so years of his life along what's now called McEntire Road. The farm is a virtual museum. A hundred yards or so beyond McEntire's broad left shoulder, near the bottom of a path that stops at the foot of a modest slope, lie the remnants of history, of eye-stinging sweat and spine-crushing work. Wheat thrashers and early tractors. Steam engines. Wheels and pulleys.

"You can see all kind of junk around here," McEntire laughs.

His boots stepping hard on loose gravel, he walks toward bins and silos where he keeps his grain. Crows squawk and songbirds counter.

The crunching footsteps slice through what is an almost unnatural quiet.

McEntire talks about the milling operation, about how easily he can transfer the corn between the bins or send it directly to his hundred-horsepower mill. "I'm proud of this," he says. "We can grind about forty-five bushels in twelve or fourteen minutes."

He packs that product in twenty-two-hundred-pound super sacks or dumps it into giant totes. McEntire grows about thirty-three acres of the heirloom corn; he grew four acres before partnering with Troy Ball. "I don't want to grow much more than that. That's all we need, as far as the blending and so forth."

He also gets white corn from Kentucky, which he blends with the

John McEntire on his farm near Old Fort. McEntire grows heirloom Crooked Creek corn for, and played a role in developing, Troy & Sons whiskeys.
Photo by NCDA&CS

Crooked Creek. He grows sorghum cane, soybeans, and the heirloom turkey red wheat.

"Let's go to the fields," he says. "What are you driving?"

He eyes the pickup and deems it acceptable for the short journey into the fields of corn and wheat. It's rough going—no place for a car.

We park on a makeshift road—mostly dirt and grass—alongside neat rows of crops near the edge of a stream. "This is the Big Crooked Creek, and I live on the Little Crooked Creek."

McEntire walks toward a field of turkey red wheat, which he planted in November, meaning about six months ago. He picks a wheat berry and rolls it between his thumb and index finger. "Still kind of soft," he says. "I hope I'm not making a mistake and leaving it."

You want firm wheat berries, he explains.

"Not quite there yet," he says, "but when it's really ready, it will almost fall out of there."

He walks into a beautiful field of tall, brilliant green corn, which grows white on a red cob. "I've got another heirloom corn I just found last winter, and they tell me, but I'm not sure about that, that it may be the last of the seeds on that corn."

Typically, Crooked Creek yields one ear per stalk. It's mid-June and so far a little dry, the result of a high-pressure "heat dome" that has encapsulated much of the country. The corn is struggling just a bit, but McEntire isn't concerned. "Just a shower of rain will bring that back."

He will be proven correct when a hot July relents to cooler temperatures and early-August rain. No worries.

"We experimented blending the turkey red wheat with the Crooked Creek corn, and made the Blonde whiskey," he says. "There's where it gets its taste, flavor, so forth. That was unique. I didn't have any idea. I knew it was good corn for grits and so forth—cornbread. I knew all the moonshiners around here liked it. We're in a conservative area, and I hate that. A lot of the neighbors, they frown on the idea of that." McEntire emphasizes "frown." He raises his voice and draws it out, for all the world sounding like Sheriff Andy Taylor in an especially preachy moment.

He knew moonshiners who worked in the woods and along the creeks. Knew them personally, he says.

"About three of them would be in church, a little Baptist church, on Sunday morning, and the preacher was just railing against the vices. They'd sit there just as staunch-faced as anybody you'd ever seen. I thought, Something's not quite right with this picture. Either you do or you don't."

A rooster crows in the distance. It's hard to tell where, way out here in nature. Bees are buzzing in the trees. McEntire turns and tilts his head back. He decides the bees are in a maple tree. No, the wild cherry tree.

He talks of planting buckwheat, to the benefit of the bees.

"I love the honeybees," he says.

Howling Moon

42 Old Elk Mountain Road
Asheville, NC 28804
howlingmoonshine.com
The distillery doesn't offer public tours
currently.

Cody Bradford of Howling Moon knows moonshine. For a long time, he has known how it's made and how it should taste. His father and extended family made it. His grandfather and his grandfather's father made it, too. Scots-Irish immigrants and those who left the hills and hollows of western Pennsylvania after the Whiskey Rebellion for the sprawling, wild, and rugged mountains of western North Carolina.

Bradford, the distillery's CEO, can trace his family's connection to moonshine to 1866 at least. "My family has done it forever, and up until recently they've all been moonshiners," he says.

He and his brother, Austin, talked of starting a business. They threw around ideas, including venturing out as hops farmers.

It's human nature to overlook the familiar in search of something else. Until we realize that what we view as commonplace is in fact extraordinary.

Moonshine.

"We had a lot of family history with it and everything, so this made a lot of sense," Bradford says.

The distillery, technically in Woodfin just north of Asheville, got its permits in late 2010. Bradford—he's partners with his brother and friend Chivous Downey—had an inkling he was on to something. "Some moonshine had come out on the market, and I tried some of it because I love moonshine, drank it my whole life, and just wanted to see what it was about in stores, and it was just vodka," he says. "That's all it was. I was, like, 'Wow, this isn't moonshine.' I tried several of them, and they were all the same.

"We make good liquor. My family made it forever. I know what it is. I'm

Brothers Austin, *left*, and Cody Bradford at their distillery in Woodfin, outside Asheville
Photo by Lisa Snedeker

just going to start making it so these people can know what real moonshine is."

The first batch of Howling Moon appeared in ABC stores in February 2012. In the busy winter season, the distillery sells as many as thirty-five thousand jars each month.

Quite the haul, so to speak.

The clear, 100-proof moonshine is made with local corn, harvested in nearby Maggie Valley, and sugarcane. Howling Moon makes an 80-proof Moonshine Whiskey, aged with oak chips. Its 100-proof all-natural flavored 'shines include peach, strawberry, and apple pie. They're burn-free and sippable, best consumed straight from the jar.

"My dad used the same recipe, and my grandfather and great-uncle used the same recipe, and my great-great-grandfather used the same recipe," Bradford says. "I know that for sure."

Howling Moon isn't hidden, but it's decidedly inconspicuous. Off a narrow road, in a plain, two-story, tan-colored block building. Stashed behind a

The partners at Howling Moon built their distillery from parts and pieces that go back decades, including this rustic, yet efficient, condenser.
Photo by Lisa Snedeker

slew of parked cars and the usual neighborhood goings-on.

To find Howling Moon, one must be looking for Howling Moon. But people find it. All the time.

People such as Norman Reedus, who plays Daryl Dixon on the AMC zombiefest *The Walking Dead*. Reedus stopped by Howling Moon for an episode of another show, *Ride with Norman Reedus*. ESPN featured the distillery in a spot during a *Monday Night Football* broadcast from Charlotte. Cast and crew from the Discovery Channel's *Moonshiners* have been here, too. Zagat was planning a visit, says Bradford, who typically doesn't open the distillery for public tours.

The distillery is unpretentious. Straightforward. If there has ever been a perfect place to make moonshine, this is it.

The partners built the distillery from parts and pieces once used to make whiskey in barns and in the woods. One still holds 750 gallons, two more about 250 gallons each. Heated with propane. A condenser—a large, hollow tube—is more than a hundred years old.

"It works a lot better than the worm, if you're trying to make a lot of liquor," Bradford says of the condenser. "With a worm, you've got to run really slow. We reconditioned and reused some of the old equipment, and then I made all of my other equipment based off the same designs my dad used, and grandparents.

"We put out a real product, and we've done really good with it. We've got a lot of recognition. I've got over a thousand gallons' worth of capacity in all my stills, and I can't keep up with North Carolina."

Bradford walks to a room beyond the stills, toward a frame holding photos of his family. He talks about Howling Moon, about how it's based on a true story. A story of a first date. Of drinking moonshine and riding horses. Of looking up and howling at the moon.

His great-great-grandfather's still is tucked away in a corner opposite the photos. The cap is missing. Bradford returns to the distillery before venturing into the steamy August afternoon to retrieve a jar of his peach moonshine from his pickup. The whiskey is warm, and he suggests chilling it for a bit. He talks about the distilling industry, about crowded shelves and a crowded and expanding moonshine market. He bemoans negative perceptions, yet is optimistic that consumers are getting smarter about their liquor.

"I'm just glad to see people do it real," he says.

H & H Distillery

204 Charlotte Highway, Suite D
Asheville, NC 28803
hhdistillery.com
828-338-9779
Call for information about tours and tastings.

JASON RIGGS IS AN ECLECTIC SORT.

Slightly built, with glasses and a mop of light brown hair, Riggs bends to check a distillate and hops back up, jumping into the conversation. His speech is frenetic, oozing passion and creativity. As he talks about science, chemistry, and distillation, he's like a motivational speaker who badly wants his listener to feel better about himself.

"I'm a little bit of a fermentation scientist," says Riggs, who also has a background in brewing. He mentions whiskey and gin, vodka. Rum, released the past summer, was first, he says. It's called Hazel 63, in honor of a 1963 Cadillac Fleetwood and Taylor Howard's grandfather, Hazel.

Taylor Howard, an engineer, is a founder of H & H Distillery in Asheville. He and his father, Wendell, are partners in the business, which got started in 2012. Because of Asheville's proximity to Hendersonville, a bastion of apples and home to an annual apple festival, Taylor envisioned an apple brandy to start.

H & H decided to go with rum, though that brandy may come later.

"The rum is from a really nice premium molasses," Riggs says. "It's a Caribbean select. I went through tedious calculations to find the right type of yeast I wanted to work with. We probably had twelve different buckets."

Riggs quickly moves from talk of yeast to talk of water. "We have really nice water chemistry here in Asheville, and the brewers will really tell you about that," he says. "It doesn't mean that we have all the nutrients in there to really go and start brewing with. It means we actually have a clean slate, so there's not a lot in there. It's more difficult to remove all those impurities than it is to actually put things back in."

Hazel 63 Rum from H & H Distillery was inspired by this 1963 Cadillac Fleetwood and named in honor of Taylor Howard's grandfather.
Photo by H & H Distillery

He directs attention to the rows of shelves lined with Mason jars, each holding a distinctive brown liquid. Some are full, others about halfway so. Some are nearly empty. An intern works on a counter under the shelves. At his feet are more containers—plastic and stainless steel.

"I've played with all the different types of wood," Riggs says. "Not only are we playing with American charred oak, but we're playing with different toast levels, as well as some French oak. What you'll see in some of our other products is that I really wanted to get this out there and be cost-effective on the shelf. We're also going to play with not only oak in the future, but with some other fruit-bearing trees—apple, cherry—and maybe even a sweet whiskey liquor with maple wood."

He calls the rum "lightly aged," through a process known as micro-oxygenation.

The Old 74 Vodka is named after the highway that runs outside the distillery, which is part of a building housing several businesses, including T & K Utilities, which Wendell Howard started. "We'll basically neutralize all the stuff we could not take for the whiskey and sell that as a vodka, which will be a nice premium vodka," says Riggs, describing the recipe as a corn and barley

Jason Riggs, a self-described "fermentation scientist," is a lead distiller for Taylor Howard and H & H Distillery in Asheville.
Photo by NCDA&CS

blend with specialty malts. "The whiskey is already in trials, and the vodka is actually a derivative of the whiskey. We will have a bourbon, but that will take many years. So, basically, I've allocated about 10 percent of my resources that come off the still to go into barrels, because we need some stuff to go out on the shelves right now, to have some cash flow. I'm going to fill every barrel I get, and then I'm going to throw some in here and oxygenate them on wood chips as well."

H & H plans to infuse a forthcoming gin with birch sap, the type soda companies use for birch beer. "We're really excited to pull that out." Riggs says it will compare more closely to a jenever, an ancestor of modern gin. "We won't completely neutralize that spirit. A lot of gins throughout the world that are produced are coming from a vodka, a GNS"—a grain-neutral spirit—"and then they put in all the botanicals after the fact—in a gin basket, for example. But I'm actually going to save some of those flavors from the birch, and I think that will really pair nicely with some of the other stuff." Rose petals and local herbs and roots. Stuff such as that.

Taylor Howard heads through the distillery, past the mash tun, the copper pot–column hybrid still. At the back of the shop, he pushes open a door, revealing a work in progress. H & H is already expanding. Workers have pushed back a dirt wall, creating a walkway that will lead to a warehouse, where, among other uses, barrels will be stored and aged. "That will free up some space where we can add another still," Howard says.

Riggs and Howard met via a mutual friend.

"I came in, and I saw this system," Riggs says. "I was like, 'Oh, crap, I really want to play with these toys.'"

Riggs takes a second to reflect, a rarity for the past hour or so. "Humble beginnings right now," he says, "but I think we're primed to do some cool stuff in here."

"It's a big investment," Howard says. "We're not scared. As long as you keep pushing."

Taylor Howard of H & H Distillery places a label his Old 74 Vodka.
Photo by NCDA&CS

Blue Ridge Distilling Co.

228 Redbud Lane
Bostic, NC 28018
defiantwhisky.com
828-245-2041
The distillery is open from 9 A.M. to 4 P.M.
Monday through Friday. Call for information about tours and tastings.

THE PUBLIC GOT ITS FIRST TASTE of Defiant Single Malt American Whisky—
no *e* here—in December 2012.

Four years later, people in twenty-eight states and five countries were enjoying this fine whiskey, distilled, as its label boasts, from 100 percent malted
barley and pure mountain spring water. At 82 proof, it tastes of caramel and
sweet vanilla. It's perfectly oaked, sweet, yet peppery, without even a tiny in-
sinuation of so-called heat or burn, much like a premium scotch aged for a
dozen or so years in an oak barrel.

The Defiant story transcends the typical whiskey odyssey. Imagination
elbows its way to the front, running through and past the dusty footsteps of
tradition and convention.

Tim Ferris seems relaxed. Wearing shorts and a slate blue Defiant Marine T-shirt, he chooses a comfortable chair in his large office, located in a loft
on the second floor of his distillery in Bostic. Defiant Marine, which Ferris
founded, provides deep-sea diving, salvage, and emergency response services
worldwide.

High stakes and highly dangerous.

"My team was in Egypt, right smack dab in the middle of the Arab
Spring," he recalls. "When that whole thing went down, we were in the thick
of it, watching, two days in, as they're stacking bodies like cordwood in the
back of flatbed trucks, all the police stations ransacked and the riot trucks
flipped over, military tanks rolling into the city, a shutdown of communications and transportation, a run on the banks."

After Hurricane Sandy wrecked a large swath of the East Coast in Octo-

Defiant American Single-Malt Whisky is an ode to Defiant Marine, a deep-sea diving and salvage company founded by Tim Ferris, who also founded the distillery.
Photo courtesy of Blue Ridge Distilling Co.

ber 2012, Ferris and his team pumped millions of gallons of water and sludge from the New York City subway system in lower Manhattan. "We were living in Battery Park, and the sun would go down and the lights would stay off. Manhattan was black, and it was unbelievable," Ferris says. "We knocked it out quick. It was high pressure. They needed it done. They needed the city back online. We got it pumped out, and the trains started to roll within about eleven days."

A nine-part series on the History Channel, *Billion Dollar Wreck*, documented Ferris and his crew as they worked to recover billions of dollars in gold that went down with the White Star liner RMS *Republic*.

All very real, he says.

Vision is a catalyst for creation and invention. "With diving and salvage, the whole name of the game is going innovative for the sake of results. It's not being innovative for the sake of innovation. It's being innovative to get a result, where there's no rules."

Whiskey production has all sorts of guidelines, rules, and regulations. Bourbon is bound by a set of rules, and so is scotch. Oak barrels are the preferred or, in the case of bourbon, required method of aging for distillers who have a long history of making whiskey. Distillers with thousands of barrels of aging whiskey stacked floor to ceiling in massive rickhouses. Distillers who can afford the luxury of patience.

Distillers who can afford to wait.

"What if you didn't make enough whiskey in 1986, and you're out?" Ferris asks. "So you've gone through all this marketing, all the sales, distributing, relationships, and then all of a sudden somebody says, 'Oh, my God, I love that vintage. Can I have about four hundred more cases?' With us, if somebody says, 'Oh, my God, we love your product. We'll order five more pallets,' we can make more and deliver it within four months."

When it came time to age his whiskey, the next step would have entailed pouring the clear product into oak barrels. Ferris reacted with a word favored by recalcitrant toddlers and people who refuse to accept the status quo.

Why?

A single word, yet a question in need of an answer.

"Why are we putting something into a vessel that is archaic technology? A barrel was never designed for aging whiskey. It never happened that way," Ferris says.

Someone discovered, he says, that oak softens and complements the whiskey, imparting complex sugars, natural tannins, and—in a charred barrel—brilliant amber tone.

"Nobody ever stopped and said, 'Okay, if a barrel has proved that there's a relationship between spirit and wood, then is the barrel the best mechanism for facilitating that marriage?' The answer is it's not, because a barrel is designed with staves that are cut like a plank for a boat hull, designed not to leak and not to be permeated or penetrated by the product.

"So we stopped and said, 'Let's not think of oak as a vessel. Let's look at oak as an ingredient.' If oak is an ingredient . . . Think of a tea, think steeping. When you take a tea bag and dip it in hot water, you get the colors of a tea, the flavors of a tea. Tea is the ingredient. It doesn't need to be the cup.

"When I approached whiskey with the philosophy of, 'Let's look at oak as another ingredient,' it was a game changer. What we found is, you can drive the extraction of all the compounds and elements that you want out of the oak, so effectively and under such control that you can maintain consistency of flavor and not have to vat multiple batches together to homogenize the palate."

Trial and error.

Innovation and invention.

Defiant uses oak spirals—the product of a pot-column hybrid still made by Kothe—to age its "whisky." Think of foot-long wooden curlicues. Each 390-gallon stainless-steel tank of whiskey is aged for sixty days using about two hundred feet of the spirals, and each tank is bottled as an individual batch. No blending or mixing.

"Each batch is its own bottling run," Ferris says. "We don't mix batch 31 and batch 32 and batch 33 to homogenize the flavor."

The wood's capillaries flood completely and quickly, the oak floating in the spirits, absorbing the whiskey by means similar to a sponge. Within ten minutes, the wood rests at the bottom of the tank.

"We don't stir it, we don't agitate, we don't mess with it. There's no tricks," Ferris says. "What we found after extensive testing—at this point, we're five years into the testing—is that at sixty days, with the method that we use, looking at oak as an ingredient, the saturation point has been reached. Meaning, if you left it for another five years on the oak, the way we use it, you're not going to get any more change. You're not going to get any darker color. You're not going to get any more oak sugar. We've gotten everything you can get in sixty days. It's not about aging, it's about maturity."

Blue Ridge Distilling Co.'s Defiant "whisky" is made in a Kothe pot-column hybrid still and aged with oak spirals, which are immersed in stainless-steel tanks.
Photo courtesy of Blue Ridge Distilling Co.

Think, Ferris says, about people with a background in commercial diving, people who breathe different mixes of gases under pressure. How they think. How they face and resolve problems regardless of how seemingly simple or excruciatingly complex.

Distillers Eric Meech and Joel Patrino use a proprietary process to finish the whiskey.

"A barrel leaks and breathes," Ferris explains. "It's not a perfect vessel. One of the things that a barrel does that's more effective than the interface between the wood and the spirit is the interface between the spirit and oxygen. Because the barrel's breathing every day, through hot and cold, and it's breathing through every season, through hot and cold.

"So we do that under our control as well. And we found that we can accelerate the process by engineering and understanding what's taking place on the chemistry basis, between oxygen and spirit, and that's how we finish the whiskey. We've divided the process to where oaking is one thing, oxygen is one thing, and Defiant is the result.

"If your goal is to brag about a twelve-year-old whiskey, we're not the right whiskey for you. If you want a whiskey that's extraordinarily drinkable and clean, Defiant's it. It's a great whiskey."

No added flavors or colors. Just barley, yeast, and oak.

Ferris gets up from his chair and walks to a desk in a corner of the room—which is reached by climbing a narrow and dizzily winding staircase. As he returns to the chair, he drops a piece of white paper on a coffee table in the center of the room.

It's his new label. For a 100 percent rye whiskey.

It's a difficult and stubborn grain, without question.

"We almost lost several hoses and a pump," Ferris says of the early rye distillations. "We made liquid nails."

But mashed and distilled correctly, it's savory and a bit sweet. Eventually, Defiant, um, nailed it.

"It's got a skin like a peanut, so when you're trying to mash it and lauter it, you have to know what you're doing," Ferris says of rye, which, like its barley, the distillery buys from Briess Malt & Ingredients Co. in Wisconsin.

The distillery rented a machine built to separate curds. It used the machine to separate rye solids from the rye wash and to "make it 100 percent malted rye, with nothing else in the mash bill at all. For rye, you've got to add a ton of rice hulls. Now, you've got another product in the mash tun. We didn't want to do that."

Joel Patrino was involved in the project from the start, as an electrician.

"He knew the systems," Ferris says. "He knew mills and the stills and the mash tuns and the control systems, because he pulls wires for all of it. He had a background in the fermentation sciences and, packing up his electrical tools, said, 'I'm ready to come on board.'"

Patrino needed help. He called Eric Meech, who was running his own charter fishing and dive company in Florida. Meech, like Patrino, knew more than a little about whiskey. "Joel called me and asked me if I wanted to move to North Carolina and work at a distillery," Meech recalls. "I said no."

Patrino persuaded Meech to travel north and take a look.

"So I drove up, walked in, saw all this shiny equipment. That proverbial 'Ahh' went off," says Meech. "So I went home, sold my business, sold all my toys, put my house up for rent, talked my wife into doing all that, and moved here."

Here is Golden Valley in the foothills of the South Mountains in western North Carolina. It's remote, accessible by gravel road, surrounded by open fields and dense, lush woods.

"We're out in the middle of nowhere, to where if you pull in the driveway, and if you've found us, you've had to look for us," Ferris says.

People have. Ferris and his team guide about four tours each day.

In late 2015, Defiant bought and transformed a 550-acre tract, a former Girl Scout camp about two miles from the distillery. There, it offers tastings and "whisky" merchandise. "Camp Golden Valley is the perfect place to expand the distillery," Ferris says. "We are quickly running out of space at our current facility, and our goal is to expand our production to the camp and develop a tourism destination comparable to distilleries on the [Kentucky] Bourbon Trail."

Some eighty pallets loaded with whiskey are rolled out of the distillery each year, a cargo that equates to about seventy thousand bottles or six thousand cases. The big distillers such as those in and around Louisville, Kentucky, produce several times as many cases. Each day. Yet by North Carolina standards, in a tough environment to sell spirits, Ferris has done well.

"I actually expected it to be more successful faster, but that was based on all my ignorance," he says. "I chose to make a product that really has no category in the U.S. American single malt. So what do they do, put you with the scotch, or do they put you with the American bourbon? There's really nothing in between. So, if I was to rewind and start over again, I would have started with the product that I still love but that was recognizable in

Tim Ferris at his distillery in Bostic
Photo courtesy of Blue Ridge Distilling Co.

a preexisting market, so we weren't fighting multiple battles."

Defiant has become successful because, regardless of what type of whiskey it is, it's good whiskey. Or, well, "whisky."

"I'm looking for somebody that already appreciates whiskey in whatever flavor it comes in—bourbon, rye, single malt," Ferris says. "I'm looking for somebody that's never tried whiskey, or maybe has had a bad experience with a more bold whiskey—you know, a harsher bourbon—and they try Defiant, and it's so drinkable, it's so smooth, and it's still complex, and they go, 'Oh, my, I like this.' And that's what we've gotten, more often than not."

Southern Artisan Spirits

405 South Cansler Street
Kings Mountain, NC 28086
southernartisanspirits.com
704-297-0191
Call the distillery for information about
tours and tastings.

ALEX AND CHARLIE MAUNEY LIKE TO BAKE.

Grains, water.

Yeast.

It was a hobby for the twin brothers, but there was something about those ingredients. How else could they use them, and what else could they make?

Rhetorical questions, really.

"It kind of started out as a bread-baking hobby and turned into a liquor-making hobby," Charlie says.

From the kitchen to the garage. From bread to vodka. From the garage to a distillery, the state's third since Prohibition. From vodka to gin.

"The vodka market was kind of saturated," Charlie says. "It was kind of a boring spirit to start with. But a lot of work goes into making it. We wanted to do something different."

The brothers and their father, Jim, formed Southern Artisan Spirits in Kings Mountain, a town of about ten thousand straddling Cleveland and Gaston Counties in the south-central part of the state. The town, the distillery's website declares, was the first in the United States to go legally dry, in October 1874.

Southern Artisan released its 84-proof Cardinal Gin—named after the state bird—in 2010, although it was a couple of years in the making. As of August 2016, the tasty gin was in ten states, including South Carolina, Georgia, Florida, Maryland, Kentucky, and Illinois. The distillery has exported some to Italy, Charlie says. "We sent a whole container load over there. That's pretty cool. We have distribution in Germany, Austria, Switzerland, France," as well as parts of Eastern Europe. "We've done pretty well with the gin."

Cardinal American Dry Gin from Southern Artisan Spirits in Kings Mountain. The distillery's signature spirit is named after the state bird.

Photo courtesy of Southern Artisan Spirits

The distillery infuses eleven botanicals into its contemporary, or modern-style, gin, which is a bit lighter on the juniper.

Southern Artisan is adding thousands of square feet to the original distillery, which it will use to store grains and racks of fifty-three-gallon American white oak barrels filled with aging rye and bourbon whiskeys, made in a thousand-gallon stripping still. The cuts come after the spirits are redistilled in a copper-pot still. "We're not trying to force it or anything," Charlie says of the aging process. "We may release a little bit of rye next year. I'm not really sure. We'll see what it tastes like then.

"We really just started setting whiskey back two months ago," he says. "We got about twenty barrels set back. This past year, we've really been putting a lot more money into equipment."

Sixty percent of the rye whiskey will be its namesake grain. It will also include a bit of corn and a rye malt, giving it a sweeter flavor.

"I'm looking forward to it," Charlie says.

The expansion will provide space for a store, tours, and tastings, which to this point haven't been part of the distillery's plans.

"It's been a struggle," Charlie says, "but I think we're starting to make a little headway."

Carolina Distillery

1001 West Avenue, NW
Lenoir, NC 28645
carolinadistillery.com
828-499-3095
Tours and tastings are offered on the hour
from noon to 5 p.m. on Friday and Saturday. Call for more information.

"I'm Hippy. Nice to meet you."

Hippy Sisk is wearing a gray T-shirt that matches his long hair and beard. Hippy isn't his given name. It's Tim, but everyone calls him Hippy. Ever since he can remember, he says.

He descends a flight of stairs leading to the basement of Carolina Distillery in Lenoir, the Caldwell County seat and a town of eighteen thousand in the foothills of the Blue Ridge Mountains, which stretch along the state's western and northern edges.

The distillery, the state's second after Prohibition, occupies a building downtown that dates to 1935 and was at one time or another home to department and discount stores, including the venerable Roses, a once-ubiquitous fixture in towns and cities throughout North Carolina.

At the foot of the steps, Sisk, the master distiller, makes a sharp turn and heads toward a far wall, where he gestures toward a pair of stainless-steel barrels, each containing about a thousand gallons of fermenting apple mash. He points to one barrel and then another—the last fermentation of the season, until the fall harvest. "This one was started yesterday, and that one's about a week old," he says. "You can see the difference in how hard they're working."

The distillery combines apples from Perry Lowe Orchards in Moravian Falls—about twenty-five miles northeast—with yeast and sugar. That's the recipe.

"We won't get any more apples until they start harvesting again," Sisk says. "We've tried other stuff, but the fresh apple juice works the best."

Tim "Hippy" Sisk checks the apple mash at Carolina Distillery in Lenoir.
Photo by John Trump

The name of Carolina Distillery's signature Carriage House Apple Brandy pays homage to the initial distillery in downtown Lenoir. Carolina also makes a strawberry-infused apple brandy made from locally sourced strawberries, unaged white apple brandy, and a slightly sweeter apple pie Carolina 'shine.

"We put it in barrels, it turns into our brown," Sisk says. "If we put in strawberries, it turns into our strawberry. And if we put it straight into our bottle, it's our white. It sits in a barrel about a year. A year's a good average. Sometimes, it's a little more. Sometimes, it's a little less. We don't have a rule because we're apple brandy. If we were straight brandy, we'd have to stay in a barrel for two years. We don't have those rules. We do whatever we want to."

And they do it well.

The aged apple brandy clocks in at around 80 proof, the white liquor at about 90 proof. Each barrel imparts unique traits to the resultant liquor. The apple is an easy sipper, smoother than bourbon on the front and leaving just a small bite at the back of the throat.

"We made a couple things. It was terrible," co-owner Keith Nordan says. "We made something else. It was terrible. Then we got to looking at the market and what was out there."

A lot of whiskey and vodka. Shelves filled with gin and rum.

"But what we didn't see was a lot of brandy," Nordan says. "Moonshiners originally made products according to what was available at the time. The fall of the year, we had fruit. The spring, we had peaches. Then we had corn or whatever in the middle."

Carolina Distillery gets its new, charred American white oak barrels from a cooperage in Kentucky, Sisk says. "You can't beat that barrel. That barrel does something to it that nothing else does."

Their first distillation, in November 2009, aged in one such barrel. Safe and quiet for most of the year.

"We only get into it at Christmas," Sisk says. "Every anniversary, November 29, everybody that was here the day it was made comes by, and we take a bottle out and sample it. It's delicious, too."

Visitors to the distillery cross the heart of the once-bustling store, now cavernous and largely empty, to reach the tasting room, which is hard to miss. This day, a representative from the state's international marketing team is hosting a buyer, who is visiting distilleries around North Carolina. A few distillers have come to Lenoir to promote their products. They gather in the tasting room, at tables and around the bar.

Nordan glances toward the still. It's quiet for now. He turns and looks through the large department-store plate-glass windows, which offer a view of downtown Lenoir, its streets, on this day in June, soaked with rain.

"We're traditional, old-school," Nordan says. "We're strictly the way they did it a hundred years ago."

A simple process.

Perry Lowe Orchards

In an orchard twenty-five miles or so northeast of Lenoir, at the end of a route that cuts between Pisgah National Forest and the South Mountains, Perry Lowe's son Ty is growing apples.

About thirty varieties. Sweet and sour. Red, green, and gold. One hundred acres and thirty-five thousand trees. Atop a summit in what's technically Moravian Falls, along the border separating Wilkes and Alexander Counties.

The Lowes are sixth-generation apple farmers, though Ty's grandfather bought the land for today's orchard in the 1940s.

The orchard has supplied apple juice—the product of a continuous belt press—to Keith Nordan and Carolina Distillery for several years. The blends include Red Delicious, Golden Delicious, Staymans, Winesaps, and Galas. Fujis, Pink Ladies, and Limbertwigs.

"What we usually do is just do our mix for him, which would be any or one variety," says Ty, who took over the orchard after his father's death.

Ty collects about fifteen hundred to three thousand gallons a month when he's producing Carriage House apple brandies. He sells to purveyors of hard cider and wine, too, and he bottles several varieties of nonalcoholic cider, which he sells in the family's retail store on Highway 16.

"We've already started harvesting some of our apples," he said in late July 2016. "So we start in July harvesting some, like the Ginger Gold, and we finish in November with Fujis, Pink Ladies, and Limbertwigs."

Ty walks along a row of shelves holding dozens of jars of sweet apple cider. He addresses the merits of the Honeycrisp and the Pink Lady, pointing to clear strains and those a little bit cloudy. If it's good for juice, it's good for brandy or hard cider.

Fresh apples bring in larger profits, but the juicing operation—and the brandy and cider byproducts—help sustain the family orchard.

Ty Lowe checks his apples for ripeness and damage, including that from insects and hail.
Photo by Lisa Snedeker

"Growing in the South has its difficulties," he says. "It would be nice to say I can grow 90 percent fresh and 10 percent processed. This year, it's going to be extremely hard to get 50 percent fresh."

At one time, 120 farmers grew and sold apples in Wilkes County, Ty says. Now, there's a dozen. He tried marketing to grocery chains, but he says there's always a middleman, "somebody taking pennies and bucks away from you."

The orchard can store up to forty thousand bushels in three storage units that can hold as many as two thousand bins in temperatures just above freezing.

"A lot of people think when you pick an apple, it's dead. But it's not. It's living. The colder you keep it, the slower it continues to ripen." He says that a cold temperature "slows the apple's respiration down, so therefore it keeps firmer and fresher longer. When you press apples, it's hard to press a soft apple, so we want a firm apple, even to press."

Ty heads into a large room filled with equipment used to wash and grade apples. It's a popular stop for students who tour the business. A large sign hangs on a side wall. Most everyone who enters the room sees it, but those who read it may miss the larger story told within the painted sign. It says, "Perry Lowe White Lightnin' Apples." A little man in one corner of the sign holds tight to a red jug, an obvious reference to the moonshining that once permeated western North Carolina.

The sign goes back to when the business was Perry Lowe and Sons—to a time when Ty's grandfather, Perry Lowe Sr., and his sons, Perry and Clyde, ran the orchard. The sign relates to a Limbertwig apple indigenous to Wilkes County. "When a researcher came to this area, he couldn't match it up with any other variety of Limbertwig, so he named it the Brushy Mountain Limbertwig," Ty says.

The orchard sits high above Highway 16 off a windy state-maintained road that becomes a winding state-maintained gravel road. Ty points to homes the family has built here. It's a popular site for hang gliders. The views of the coves and valleys are stunning.

He walks along the rows of trees, inspecting, picking. He points out an apple dented by hail, which crashed down a few weeks earlier. That apple will probably become juice. He finds others with similar damage.

Deer eat leaves, an act that does more damage than eating the fruit. The pesky codling moth stings apples, making them "wormy." Ty traps the moths. Cameras and fences help him control other perpetrators.

"In the South, you have to really, really watch out for summer diseases, rots in particular," he says. "A rotten apple ain't even good for brandy."

He sprays as little as he can, but it's necessary nonetheless. "Organic's impossible," he says. "That's a farce in North Carolina. It cannot be done. And if it was, it wouldn't be any more healthier than what we do."

Apples litter the ground. Workers removed many of these from the trees to allow space for others to grow.

He walks to a tree of Pink Ladies. "Notice how much bigger they are because they're not competing as much for size."

Ty uses about ten pickers. Five pickers, he says, can fill four hundred to five hundred bins with Pink Ladies in around two weeks.

"If everything came in at one time, I'd pull my hair out."

He stops to grab an apple. He takes a big bite, declaring it delicious. A little green and a bit starchy, he says. He finishes it and tosses away the core.

He sighs and laments the hail damage. Crop insurance will help, he says. "What we try to do is just stay from one year to the next."

He heads toward his truck. He's expected for a family reunion, and he's already pushing time at the seams. He opens the door, heads to the highway, and takes a left. The view is tremendous.

Laws Distillery

Lenoir, NC
Tours and tastings are not offered.

A few centuries ago, distillers determined the strength of their liquor by throwing in some gunpowder and setting it ablaze. The alcohol content for liquor that failed to light was deemed too low, meaning it contained less than 57 percent alcohol. Thus, the origin of *proof*.

Yellow flames weren't good either, as they indicated the alcohol content was too high, making the liquor dangerous to drink. What distillers wanted was a lingering blue flame, which meant they had hit the proverbial mark.

Jimmy Laws was thinking about what to call his new legal whiskey. The name, he says, just came to him. And it was perfect: Still Blue.

"If you've seen my bottle, if you've seen my flames, that's what I'm all about, how pretty mine burns. How good it burns," Laws says.

In 2014, Laws obtained a permit to distill liquor. He was already quite familiar with the process. He grinds his corn in a stone mill. He distills in a copper pot—never a column—that he made himself. His distillery is deep in the woods, where hills converge. Where foothills become mountains.

"My recipe's mine. I had to learn everything. I poured my own concrete. I built my own building. I had to learn how to weld copper myself.

"You can't see inside of a liquor still. It's a magical thing. Alcohol will come before steam. It's as damned pure as you can get. I think I have some of the best water there is in this country."

Laws doesn't offer tours and tastings. He's not a fan of TV shows and movies about moonshiners or mountain men, doesn't care for smartphones or search engines. He doesn't see the appeal of brown whiskey and questions the idea of aging liquor in oak barrels.

Just not his way.

It all may seem a bit strange until you talk to him. Until you drink his clean and smooth 90-proof whiskey.

Jimmy Laws distills Still Blue Whiskey—"Still Cooked The Old Fashion Way."
Photo courtesy of Laws Distillery, Inc.

"People keep talking about why it's so smooth and why it's so good and why it's so potent," Laws says. "I said, 'Well, I'm pretty sure I'm doing something that nobody's ever done.' I've never heard tell of it done. I don't even put it on my bottle.

"It made my stuff a lot better, a lot smoother. I'm not bragging, but I think it's the best out there, and there's a lot of people waiting until I do put it in an oak barrel. I don't want it in an oak barrel, but I may. You're not going to change American people and how they think.

"I never met anyone who didn't like it. I hope they enjoy it, and when you do get to drinking, let somebody else drive."

It could be because of the spring water, the way he grinds his corn, or the way he built his still. Or maybe something else entirely. Laws is smart, funny, and engaging. He understands that offering tours and tastings could add profit to his business, but he pushes that idea aside.

Just not his way.

He's often frustrated by the ABC system, by the rules, restrictions, and requirements. But it's okay, he says. He's confident in his product, as he should be.

"It ain't about money to me. It's been fun so far, and I ain't going to let them take the fun out of it."

Foothills Distillery

300 Thornburg Drive SE, Suite A
Conover, NC 28613
seventeentwelvespirits.com
828-381-2949
Tours and tastings are offered at noon,
1 P.M., and 2 P.M. each Saturday.

SEVENTEEN TWELVE SOUTHERN SPIRITS introduced North Carolina's first bourbon since Prohibition on October 1, 2015, says Zackary Cranford, distiller and founder of Foothills Distillery, which manufactures the spirits. It was the same day distilleries began selling their products on-site—one bottle per customer per year, according to state law.

Seventeen Twelve, named for the year North and South Carolina became separate states, got its license in the spring of 2014. Cranford, one of the state's youngest distillers, says he wrote the business plan while a student at North Carolina State University in Raleigh.

In working for a local brewer, he noted that the state had more breweries than it had counties. A lot more.

"I started to look in a different direction," he says. "I found out the distilling industry was very, very young, the craft aspect of it. I wrote a business plan to see if it was even feasible, and it turns out it was. Everything kind of started lining up in that regard."

He got together with veteran distiller Tim Weaver, and they hooked up with Catawba County farmer Russell Hedrick to conceive Gatlin 110, a high-proof and, as the distillery's website says, "a straight-shooting clear whiskey with a mild undertone followed by a late kick reminiscent of the recoil from a [G]atling gun."

Products of North Carolina agriculture—yellow corn, malted barley, and rye—comprise the mash bill.

"We wanted something as authentic as possible," Cranford says. "Something

Seventeen Twelve Southern Spirits founder Zackary Cranford walks visitors on a tour of the Conover distillery.
Photo by Lisa Snedeker

that you would get from the back of a car on Highway 16," a reference to the north-south corridor that traverses western North Carolina and bisects Conover, a town of about eight thousand less than ten miles east of Hickory. "This was our bridge to start getting sales until we released our bourbon."

The distillery is right off the highway in a plain industrial building. A place where people make things. It's one of the hottest days of one of the hottest North Carolina summers on record. A good-sized exhaust fan, set in front of an open door at the far end of the building, rumbles and groans. Its work seems unnecessary, because it doesn't feel as if it's making much difference. A couple is waiting for a tour, which Cranford offers each Saturday. A pair of women arrive minutes later.

Cranford starts the tour, which, counting himself, includes seven sweaty people. He reaches into a large sack and pulls out a handful of yellow corn, a varietal with large kernels and, consequently, high starch content. He grabs some wheat, some rye.

"We get our grains seven miles from the distillery," says Cranford, speaking of Hedrick's farm. Seventeen Twelve mills the non-GMO grains either the day before or the day of mashing. "You grind the grains right before you go in there"—to the mash tun and the stripping still—"the fresher it's going to taste. It's a little rugged. It's not big. It's not shiny. We're proud of that."

Cranford quizzes the group about the ratio of grain to water needed for a run—250 gallons of water and around 750 pounds of grain, dumped from a one-ton sack.

The distillery finishes its base liquor in a column still that has four copper plates. A brewing pot of coffee becomes a metaphor for the process of separating heads, hearts, and tails. The first drops are the strongest, but instead of allowing it into the pot, "we yank it out," Cranford says.

The tour has come full circle—literally, a giant clockwise loop around the distillery. Bags of grain on one side, stills and fermenters on the other. Stacks of barrels separate the distillery and the tasting bar, where the visitors will sip bourbon and white whiskey, including a wheat-based white "Carolina" whiskey that Seventeen Twelve makes for Old Nick Williams Company.

Established in 1768 and later a victim of Prohibition, Old Nick Williams was once an industry stalwart. In a bid to return to prominence, the distillery's heirs are rebuilding it about sixty miles to the east. "Our products are old family recipes and are produced with local quality grains with the same love and craftsmanship like our family has done for hundreds of years," the distillery's Zeb Williams said in an email. He expects the distillery to open around March 2017. Cranford will serve Old Nick at the tasting bar, alongside Seventeen Twelve's two fine offerings.

The bottling line at Seventeen Twelve, as is the case with most of the state's distilleries, is comprised of a group of beer-drinking and pizza-eating friends and relatives. A woman on the tour wants in on the party. When it's cooler.

"Not many people can say they bottled their own spirit," Cranford says. "And it helps us out."

The group heads to the tasting bar on the other side of the barrels, which are filled with bourbon and aging whiskey from Old Nick Williams.

Cranford figures the next batch of his bourbon will have aged about thirteen months. "When we first started, there was a barrel shortage. It took us eight months to get our first barrel. I think a lot of that was the big boys buying all the barrels, and then hurting the small guys." The distillery fills eight barrels a month, he says.

In a nod to Prohibition days, one might assume there's a secret barrel

Zackary Cranford offers visitors a taste of his products, which include
North Carolina's first bourbon since Prohibition.
Photo by Lisa Snedeker

somewhere in the distillery, stacked high or maybe low. Behind the bar or
under it. Where?

Cranford is behind the bar, pouring the three spirits into small souvenir
cups that carry the distillery logo. "These are the first drops of Old Nick in
over a hundred years," he says.

The tourists, who look as though they've just finished a 5K run, are
refreshed by the spirits, poured warm and neat. The high-proof Seventeen
Twelve white whiskey has some heat. Cranford advises that if they buy some,
they may want to mix it in place of vodka or tequila.

Oh, the secret barrel? No such barrel exists, he says between pours. Not
yet, anyway. "We're just trying to fill them as fast as we can, because we're selling them as quick as we can make them."

He saves the bourbon for last. "Y'all enjoy."

Muddy River Distillery

1500 River Drive
Belmont, NC 28012
muddyriverdistillery.com
336-516-4190
Tours and tastings are offered. Call the
distillery or check the website for
information.

ROBBIE DELANEY OF MUDDY RIVER DISTILLERY in Belmont is admiring his stills, which he built from money he earned and saved. The nearly identical stills he and his wife, Caroline, use to make their exceptional rum.

He sees them just about every day, working them for eighteen hours three or four days a week to produce three hundred to four hundred bottles.

Sparkling helmets and columns, meticulously polished copper? Stainless steel buffed to glisten like chrome? Nope, not here. Yet works of art nonetheless.

Stills, no matter how shiny and pretty, are machines. Utilitarian and pragmatic. Artists name their paintings. Delaney, who attended East Carolina University, named his stills Liberty and Democracy. They're fitting names in just about any context but especially here, in a place where craftsmen distill spirits, a process that for centuries has helped shape cultures, sparked rebellion, and encouraged trade. They're an ode to ingenuity and creation.

Muddy River has no investors. "We take all the money that we make and reinvest it into the company," Caroline says. The Delaneys recycle and reuse—things such as old dairy tanks and control boxes once used in a textile mill. "Even our mixer came out of a yarn-dyeing mill in South Carolina."

The Delaneys have encased a condenser in glass, offering a voyeuristic view of a nascent batch from the oldest rum distillery in the state. "It's also extremely efficient, too," Robbie says.

They bought a reflux column, but "through the first year of using it, we've drilled holes in it and reworked the plate formats. It works like that one."

That is, the other column. The one Robbie made. "I still think that one tastes better, but that's just because we built that one. It's all in my head."

Robbie, who has a background in construction and historic renovation, began making rum in his kitchen as a favor for a friend. The results were mixed. "We really didn't make anything worth drinking in the kitchen, so he continued to buy his Captain Morgan."

The Delaneys continued making rum. Muddy River released its first product, Carolina Rum, in 2012. The distillery moved in October 2013 into an old textile mill that sits on the bank of the Catawba River, across the parking lot from a winsome new marina. The location is about fifteen miles west of Charlotte in Gaston County. Muddy River shares the old mill with several businesses, including a brewery and a cabinet shop.

As ABC stores began stocking silver Carolina Rum, Muddy River began placing its clean new product in fifty-three-gallon virgin barrels. Rum is often aged in used barrels—barrels that once held bourbon, for example.

The 80-proof silver, which starts with molasses produced from sugarcane grown in Florida and Louisiana, is the base for all of Muddy River's spirits, including a spiced rum and a coconut-infused rum that entered the market in 2015. The Delaneys do some contract distillation as well, making a line of 'shines under the Paw Paw Murphy's label.

Muddy River introduced the aged reserve Queen Charlotte a couple of years ago. The current stock has aged about a year, but the Delaneys have plans. "We're very proud of everything we make, but Queen Charlotte, when you think of craft and small batch, that's what you're thinking of," Robbie says. "It competes with anything else that's out there. I think all of our rums are comparable with the competition, but Queen Charlotte is amazing."

And it will continue aging, in the virgin barrels that define the distillery, along the walls and against the rails that delineate the main floor from the basement, which is crowded with totes loaded with ferment.

No matter how hard or long Robbie works on a batch, no matter how careful the fermentation or tedious the cuts, Caroline has the final say. Always. "Caroline, by the way, is our secret weapon," Robbie says. "When it all comes down to it, the characteristic of the rum, it comes from the quality control."

Robbie has neatly placed several tanks of high-test rum perpendicular to the stills. He'll open them to let them breathe. It's up to Caroline to decide if they'll proceed on what's now an uncertain path to bottles.

Some say a woman's sense of smell is more acute than a man's. A study

Robbie Delaney of Muddy River Distillery in Belmont talks about his line of rums, led by the aged reserve Queen Charlotte.
Photo by NCDA&CS

in 2014 by a team led by Professor Roberto Lent of the Institute of Biomedical Sciences at the Federal University of Rio de Janeiro seemed to prove as much. "New research," reported the website medicalnewstoday.com, "shows that women have more cells in the olfactory bulb—the area of the brain that is dedicated to sense of smell—than men. The authors of the study . . . suggest this may explain why women are reported to have a better sense of smell than men."

Robbie already knew it. "Most people don't realize that, but that's the truth. That's how it works." He looks at the tanks and takes a deep breath. "I think all of this is good liquor," he says. "She might very well turn every drop of it down, making my eighteen-hour day worthless. Or she might say some of this is good, some of this is not good, so she's responsible for that."

He looks at the stills, his eyes moving slowly from Liberty to Democracy, from Democracy to Liberty. "We need another machine. It's long, long weeks for us."

The Delaneys are happy to stay close to home, so to speak. The rum does well in ABC stores in the county next door—and there are twenty-six of those.

Oak barrels filled with aging rum at Muddy River Distillery
Photo by NCDA&CS

"There's enough rum drinkers just in Mecklenburg County to make this place twice its size. We don't need to grow throughout the Southeast," Robbie says. "We do that very intentionally. We get a lot of requests from other states, and we catalog those for future reference, but as far as we're concerned, at our size—400 bottles a day, 350 bottles a day—we really can't go to other states successfully. If I was in fifteen states, I'd need a still ten times the size of the still in that room."

Robbie walks away to answer a phone call. He's waiting for a shipment of bottles, has been for most of this morning. Delivery times can be erratic, which doesn't mesh with the frenetic pace of the busy distillery. The bottles are here, he says, but he wants to show off something first.

He lifts an end of the wooden tasting bar. It takes some effort to slide it partway off the large barrel supporting it. Most everybody has a secret barrel, he says. This is his.

"It's just amazing, and that barrel's only six months old. But this will never be emptied—not in my lifetime, at least.

"If you're a good person, that's what heaven smells like when you die."

The "One-Bottle Law"

Troy Ball got her first taste of North Carolina politics several years ago.

She would have preferred to spit it back out.

Ball had played an integral role in an earlier effort to loosen ABC laws in North Carolina to allow distilleries to sell their products on-site. The bill ultimately failed, and she blames politics. "They weren't thinking about what's good for North Carolina and what's good for North Carolina businesses and what's good for North Carolina tourism," she says.

A big boost came with House Bill 909, which Governor Pat Mc-Crory signed into law in June 2015. State Representatives Mike Hager and John Bell, both Republicans, had filed the original version of that bill two months earlier. It finally made its way to the governor's desk that summer and became effective in October.

The law allows distillers "to sell spirituous liquor distilled at the distillery in closed containers to visitors who tour the distillery for consumption off the premises if the distillery manufactures less than 100,000 proof gallons per year. . . . Consumers purchasing spirituous liquor under this subdivision are limited to purchasing, and the selling distillery is limited to selling to each consumer, no more than one bottle of spirituous liquor per 12-month period." The voluminous bill also specifies a 30 percent excise tax on spirituous liquor sold in ABC stores, in addition to freight and bailment charges and the ABC markup.

Among distillers, the law has been received with varying degrees of excitement and reticence. Some laud the changes, while others say the law is mostly perfunctory, though it opens the way for shops to sell hard cider and unfortified wine in growlers.

Laws for North Carolina distilleries are especially restrictive when compared to statutes that apply to breweries and wineries, which can offer tastings, hold special events, and sell a variety of their products on-site. An effort in 2016 to allow distillers to sell one bottle of each of their products per customer per year failed.

The number of bottles any distiller can actually sell doing it one bottle at a time is contingent upon a variety of factors. Distillery location is especially key. For instance, millions visit Manteo and Nags Head each year, which means the guys at Outer Banks Distilling sell a lot of Kill Devil Rum to thirsty tourists. Scott Smith is an owner at Outer Banks Distilling, which probably leads the state in drop-in tours and, subsequently, impulse sales. "That one bottle per year, we've gone through a lot," he says. "Not sure what the other guys in the state are doing, but we do about 175 bottles a week out of here." Conversely, Covington Spirits may very well make "the Best Yam Vodka on Earth," as its slogan suggests, but the crowds have yet to converge on tiny Snow Hill.

Before the law passed, scheduling and hosting tours took distillers' time—time their staffs could have better used producing and marketing their liquor or just being with their families. "We do tours on appointment, but I don't think we've sold our first bottle" at the distillery, says James "Jimbo" Eason, who sells and markets the sweet-potato-based spirits for Covington. "I don't know if it's ever going to be a big deal for us."

For Muddy River Distillery in Belmont west of Charlotte, the law allowed owners Robbie and Caroline Delaney to hire some help.

John Benefiel and his partners at Raleigh Rum Company appreciated the new law but were dubious about any positive monetary effect, at least at first. "It was not such a big deal for us," Benefiel says. "We're like, 'Oh, one bottle?' But when you really think about it, now I've got you coming in, and I've got this group of people here. Before the law, we would do the tour, we'd give you drinks, and we'd be, like, 'Go to your ABC store. Go buy it.' How many people are really going to leave directly from here and go to the ABC store?"

Before the one-bottle law, says Donald Walton Jr., president of Walton's Distillery in Jacksonville, people became agitated when he told them no. "They would actually be upset that we couldn't sell it. They didn't understand," Walton says. "I'm not competing with the ABC system. I'm a part of it."

Even today, the state prohibits online liquor sales, so distillery owners determined to sell online do so via out-of-state distributors, meaning the tax revenue stays out-of-state as well.

Tim Ferris, who founded Defiant Marine and Blue Ridge Distilling Co., both in the town of Bostic, says North Carolina lawmakers effectively hamper one of the state's fastest-growing industries. "My dad used to say, 'They tie you hand and foot, then shoot you because you can't dance.' It's archaic."

Ferris isn't happy with how the state controls liquor sales. He's especially candid, refreshingly blunt.

"It's a struggle every day. I've dumped millions of dollars into this. This quarter was the first quarter in six years that we've shown a profit, and it's not much of a profit. If I didn't have another business to be able to finance this, we wouldn't survive. At a certain point, you throw enough wet blankets on a hot passion, you're going to extinguish it."

Bill Owens of the California-based American Distilling Institute can't help agreeing. "The control states handcuff you," he says.

On the other hand, Top of the Hill Distillery's Esteban McMahan says the new law "is a really good start to setting up a better system for North Carolina distillers to succeed. We sell a lot of stuff. It's one bottle at a time, but the important thing is we're putting a bottle in someone's hands to take home. Selling T-shirts is great, but you really want to sell your spirits."

Doc Porter's Craft Spirits

232 East Peterson Drive
Charlotte, NC 28217
docporters.com
704-266-1399
The distillery offers mini-tours and tastings from 6 P.M. to 8 P.M. on Friday and from 2 P.M. to 7 P.M. on Saturday. Owner-guided tours are available as well. Call or check the website for more information.

It's about four on a Friday afternoon. The small parking lot at Doc Porter's, nearly empty an hour ago, begins to fill. People leave their air-conditioned cars and step into the bright, humid June day, the typical transformation from warm spring to stifling summer.

The surrounding distilleries and breweries have brightened this once-industrial Charlotte neighborhood—Lower South End or, to many, LoSo. Not everyone is sold on the nickname. Some like Queen Park, the name of an old drive-in theater and the famous sign that promoted it. None of that matters, at least right now. It's Friday, the week all but forgotten after that first sip of beer. Olde Mecklenburg Brewery and Sugar Creek Brewing are quite busy, as is The Broken Spoke, a bar dovetailing with Great Wagon Road Distilling Company.

Things are a bit different down at Doc Porter's. People leaving the heat of the parking lot appreciate the respite as they enter the cool, hip tasting room. Andrew and Liz Porter, who own the distillery, warmly greet their guests before leading them into the machine works, where it's a bit hotter, a bit less comfortable.

It makes sense, really. There's work to be done. It's time to bottle the gin—batch number 3—and the people whose cars now fill the parking lot are the volunteers. The Porters, parents of two girls—one very new and the other approaching toddler status—are glad for the help.

Things are bound to be busy.

Andrew Porter, founder of Doc Porter's Craft Spirits in Charlotte
Photo by Lisa Snedeker

Andrew Porter uses thirteen botanicals in his 88-proof gin. But as friends and family work the bottling line, dispensing the gin four bottles at a time, something's going on behind them, in barrels stacked on racks along a far wall.

Bourbon is aging. Andrew says it's coming along nicely but needs more time. He's using small barrels—fifteen and twenty-five gallons—to accelerate aging and intensify interaction with the oak. Proper aging, he says, takes three years in fifty-three-gallon barrels—which most of the big Kentucky distilleries use—eighteen months or so in twenty-five-gallon barrels, and about a year in fifteen-gallon barrels.

Because of the smaller casks, whiskey entering the twenty-five-gallon barrels is about 60 percent, while that in the fifteen-gallon barrels is 57.5. "The smaller the barrel, the lower the proof you want to put in there," he says. "You do run the risk of over-oaking on a lot of these if you age too long." The whiskey, in that scenario, travels deeper into the wood and extracts the bitter tannins.

Doc Porter's bourbon mash bill is 60 percent corn, 30 percent wheat, and 10 percent malted barley. All of the grains are sourced from Tar Heel farmers. The distillery goes through about six thousand pounds of grain each month. The corn and wheat arrive in two-thousand-pound "super sacks," the malted barley in fifty-pound bags.

"We mill everything on-site," Andrew says. "It gets stuff dusty, but it's kind of worth it to get the freshest grains possible. So we use our hammer mill over here to do about five hundred pounds in an hour and a half. It's important to us to use all North Carolina products, to do everything under one roof."

The wheat and corn come from a farm in Marshall, the malted barley from Asheville.

Grain-to-glass.

The distillery employs two-thousand-gallon tanks to ferment the mash. The bourbon mash, for instance, is fermented at a temperature that hovers around thirty degrees Celsius. "I'm trying to control the fermentation temperature so we get the right blend of flavors every time we produce," Andrew says. "It's really important for us to control the fermentation temperatures."

Doc Porter's uses steam injection to power a copper pot still and a hybrid column still, part of a system designed to produce a variety of products including bourbon, gin, vodka, and, eventually, rye whiskey.

The distillery, which opened in 2015, pays homage to Andrew's grandfather, who practiced medicine in Colorado and passed away several years ago. "He's kind of who I attribute my love for science to," says Andrew, a chemical engineer who works, as does his wife, a full-time job outside the distillery. "We have a lot of scientists, engineers in this family. That's kind of why I named it after him."

Andrew grew up in New Jersey making home brew with his father, a mechanical engineer. He enjoys cooking, too. After earning a degree from Clemson University and moving to Charlotte in 2009, he decided to make something delicious.

"I was amazed there was only one brewery, Olde Mecklenburg. I thought, *Man, this is ridiculous. I'm going to open a brewery.* But I was in no position to open a brewery because I was twenty-two years old. Then, all of a sudden, breweries exploded. I was, like, *There's room for a craft distillery.* I'm more passionate about craft sprits, but I never thought it was actually something you could do. When people already know about craft beer, it's easy for them to make the jump to craft spirits and say, 'Oh, it's possible to make alcohol here, too. It's not just limited to Kentucky or other places like that.'"

Doc Porter's is named after Andrew Porter's late grandfather, Dr. Richard "Doc" Porter, a navy veteran.
Photo by Lisa Snedeker

The 80-proof vodka Andrew makes at Doc Porter's is composed solely of wheat, also grown in North Carolina. The distillery's rigorous attention to detail produces a rich vodka that conveys prominent notes of caramel and warm butterscotch, characteristics that occur naturally through grain fermentation.

"We really wanted to honor the wheat, to let the wheat character come through," Andrew says. "We wanted to use just one grain so we could kind of hone in on the subtle flavors. Then, when we do the cuts"—separating heads, hearts, and tails—"we're really strict, and we can leave in this kind of, like, caramel, butterscotch, vanilla. And we don't have to overfilter it to get rid of all the unwanted flavors. That's why we chose a single grain for the vodka.

"It's allowing a little bit of those other chemicals that are produced naturally during fermentation to come through, instead of just being 100 percent ethanol. If you're in the business of making grain-neutral spirits, then why go through the trouble of making your own vodka just to make it taste like we bought it from someone else?"

Andrew put in a lot of work before he was satisfied with his gin. He started with individual distillations on a one-liter still "to learn how they tasted individually. Out of that, I made a bunch of different trial recipes of gin," he says.

None of the herbs or botanicals played off their counterparts. Too muddled.

He kept at it, going spicier, more herbal. He added more citrus. Less citrus.

"The first thing I did was mix all my favorite ones, and that was just terrible. Then I took those, and I was able to hone it in. So this was actually the 'Gin 5.2.'"

Andrew incorporates orange and grapefruit, which are infused via their peels, sans any pith.

That's quite the story.

"We used to go and just buy fresh oranges and grapefruits, and I'd just peel the very exterior, because you don't want any of the pith, the bitterness," he says. "I was eating oranges and grapefruits all week because I'd need, like, thirty oranges and forty grapefruits" for a batch.

Porter, a former track athlete who is tall and athletic, was no doubt getting enough vitamin C. He was safe from scurvy, and his aversion to waste is commendable. But clearly, it was time to seek alternatives. It turned out that a nearby vegan restaurant that offered fresh juices was juicing the citrus and discarding the peels.

Hmm.

"We teamed up with them," Andrew says. "They juiced oranges and grapefruits early in the morning, and I just brought the peels over here."

Issue resolved.

Great Wagon Road Distilling Company

227 Southside Drive
Charlotte, NC 28217
gwrdistilling.com
704-469-9330
Tours are offered on the hour from 1 P.M. to 4 P.M. on Saturday. For more information, contact tours@gwrdistilling.com.

Doc Porter's and Great Wagon Road Distilling Company are neighbors, separated by three or four figurative football fields.

It's late Friday afternoon, and finding a place to park in Charlotte's LoSo—or Queen Park—is a challenge. The Broken Spoke, a bar separated from Great Wagon Road by a steel door and a secret combination, isn't quite full. But it's getting there. Bartenders pour craft beers—including some from LoSo neighbor Olde Mecklenburg—and servers whisk them away. Other servers leave the kitchen with sandwiches spilling over with smoked pork and brisket, with meat pies and paninis.

Ollie Mulligan, who owns the bar and Great Wagon Road Distilling Company, walks into the bar and makes a sharp left. He introduces himself, though it really isn't necessary. He's tough to miss, to ignore. Mulligan is a native of County Kildare in Ireland, and his accent is pleasant and welcoming. Dressed in a lime green polo shirt and khaki shorts, Mulligan is a hard guy not to like.

He orders a beer and begins talking.

Mulligan starts with a story of his grandfather Patrick Quinn of Cartron Drumlish, Ireland, who in 1954 was charged with a number of offenses related to making whiskey. Well, "poteen," specifically. Stories about the raid are framed and hanging on a wall in the distillery.

The vigilant Drumlish Gardai, or police, the story says, "scotched" certain illegal celebrations "on the eve of Christmas Eve" on a farm in Cartron

Ollie Mulligan, founder of Great Wagon Road Distilling Company in Charlotte, talks about his state-of-the-art still, made by German manufacturer Kothe.
Photo by Lisa Snedeker

"at the foot of Cairn Hill, and seized the poteen, a still, a worm, a cooler and a quantity of malt."

Mulligan reads it aloud and laughs. He clarifies the pronunciation: *puut-cheen.*

"It was always in the back of my mind to do something like this," he says. Making whiskey, not getting arrested. "I was just always interested in it. Of course, I like whiskey, I like drinking it."

He thinks about his grandfather.

"There's a lot of things you can make better than you can buy. Home-made pies are always better than store-bought pies. I decided to see if that was the same with whiskey. And it turned out that it is."

He laughs again, the type of laughter that's infectious, that happens among old friends. The sort of friends with whom you'd have a few beers.

Or the sort of friends who talk about applying for visas to go to the United States.

Despite the talk, none of his friends sent an application. Mulligan sent eight, on his own and their behalf, and came away with six green cards. Mulligan used one of those, a friend the other. He began his American life in Charlotte, where he had family, and over the years lived in South Carolina, California, and Florida. He eventually returned to Ireland but stayed only a couple of years. He returned to the United States for a job in Texas.

But his mind often wandered to whiskey. Golden brown, rich, and smooth.

He started distilling with a small electric still in Pineville, North Carolina, in a building about ten miles due south from Great Wagon Road. He opened the distillery and bar in Charlotte in 2015.

Mulligan guides visitors along a wall just beyond the locked door, past the newspaper clippings and toward the still, made by German manufacturer Kothe. The afternoon sun pouring through a floor-to-ceiling window intensifies the gleam of the polished copper. Mulligan admires his still, which arrived fourteen months after he ordered it. He looks at it much like a car lover would stare at a pristine 1964 Corvette. Taking it all in.

"It's a beaut," he says. "There's such craftsmanship involved in it."

One of the dozens of barrels Ollie Mulligan has stocked away at Great Wagon Road
Photo by Lisa Snedeker

Great Wagon Road's offerings include an aged single-malt, a vodka, and an un-aged whiskey.
Photo by Lisa Snedeker

He points to the copper whiskey helmet, which resembles an ornate piece of blown glass. "There's only two guys in the factory who can make it," Mulligan says. No rivets, seams, or welds. "When it was on the floor, I walked around it with a camera, and it's almost perfectly symmetrical. It's a little bit dirty now. We had a few splashes," he says, his voice rising with excitement. "It took us awhile to get the swing of it, because I'll show you the still we were using up until we got this, which was a very manual, stay-up-with-it-all-night kind of still."

Mulligan attended Spirits Institute Puget Sound in Seattle to learn more about distilling. He also got this advice: *Find a brewery that will do all of the mashing for you.*

He called on John Marrino, who founded Olde Mecklenburg Brewery, which focuses on German-style beers. Marrino is a LoSo neighbor. Mulligan says Marrino told him he would "give it a go."

Mulligan uses 100 percent pale pilsner barley malt for his Rua—Gaelic for *red*—the distillery's American single-malt whiskey, aged in twenty-five-gallon white oak barrels from Kentucky. "I made some experiments, and it turns out to be an excellent malt for a single-malt whiskey. The pale pilsner, you could just taste the beautiful burn of the whiskey, and you can just taste all that oak in it. It doesn't have a whole lot of funny business going on."

Mulligan says, "When I want to do a run of Rua, and I need a barley mash done," someone at Olde Meck "types it in, it comes out of the silos, he weighs and mashes it, and I collect it. It's been a good neighbor to have, you know."

The first releases of Rua were the product of an electric still, which Mulligan used before he got his new pride and joy, which is powered by steam. "I wanted to be the first to have something like that, so I needed to get whiskey in wood as quickly as I could," he says. What took four days on the electric still now takes just six and a half hours.

The whiskey ages, Mulligan says a bit facetiously, as long as he can stand it. "The first release was nine months because we had a blistering hot summer here, and the subsequent release was about a year."

Great Wagon Road also makes a vodka, called Ban—Gaelic for *white*—and a clear "Carolina whiskey" Mulligan calls Drumlish Poteen.

The Great Wagon Road was the trail settlers from Philadelphia took "to make it into this neck of the woods, the I-85 back in the day," he says. "All the Scots-Irish and Germans came down that way, so that's why there's moonshine in the Appalachians. It's synonymous with immigration. Like myself."

Mulligan walks from barrel to barrel. Those barrels are starting to fill what is by North Carolina standards an expansive distillery. According to a post on its Facebook page, Great Wagon Road has begun aging some of its whiskey in fifty-three-gallon barrels as well.

Mulligan nods at a group of barrels, batch number 7, "just coming up to a little over a year." He points to the date on another barrel, which was filled on a leap-year day, February 29. "It's an expensive outlay of cash, to buy all those barrels and have them sit there for a year, but you can really taste it in the product.

"This is going to be wall-to-wall barrels," says Mulligan, an arm extended, spanning the distillery.

And Mulligan's fine whiskey will age in those barrels.

For as long as he can stand it.

Seven Jars Distillery

6148 Brookshire Boulevard
Charlotte, NC 28216
sevenjars.com
704-919-0278
Call or visit the website for information
about tours.

SEVEN JARS DISTILLERY IS A RELATIVE NEWCOMER to the blink-or-you'll-miss-it chase to produce and sell spirits in North Carolina. Yet the distillery's story, so rich and unique, might never have been told. It could have remained buried deep in the Piedmont's red clay soil, if not for a little digging.

Del Ratcliffe and his mother, Velma, wanted the recipes, which had been hidden away for years on their property. Frank Ratcliffe, Del's father and Velma's husband, had buried them years ago, appropriately packaged in seven Mason jars, all wrapped tightly in aluminum foil.

Frank Ratcliffe was a bootlegger, a line of work he continued to pursue years after Prohibition, which ended in places throughout the United States but clung to life in North Carolina. The clandestine operation worked like this: Frank bought legal liquor, complete with tax stamps, disguised it, trucked it into Charlotte, and distributed it to thirsty customers.

By 1937, North Carolina began the process of legalizing liquor, and Frank's business, along with the last remnants of Prohibition, evaporated. He opened a nightclub, Friendly City Club at 110 West Sixth Street in what is now trendy Uptown Charlotte. It's where Frank met Velma, whom he hired as a singer for two weeks. They married several weeks later and, as Del says, "lived happily ever after" until Frank's death in 1977.

One night not so long later, Velma came to Del, who was about eighteen. His father had buried something out there on the property, she told him. They needed to find it. She insisted they dig at night.

"Mother didn't want anyone to know about it," Del says.

The duo dug. Then again and again. Nothing.

Rum made with blackstrap molasses was among the first offerings from Seven Jars Distillery in Charlotte.
Photo courtesy of Seven Jars Distillery/sevenjarsdistillery.com

The family sold the property in 1984. Before the closing, Del determined to give it one more try. He procured some heavy tools and, with his mother marking the way with a flashlight, got to work. "I told her, 'I'm going to go out, and I don't care if I have to dig up the whole yard to find it.'"

Del dug, and his mother swung the flashlight, at first slowly, deliberately. Suddenly, the flashes became frenetic, yet focused. Something shiny dazzled in the light—the foil-wrapped jars, filled with handwritten notes. "Daddy had accumulated all his knowledge and experience," Del says.

Velma died in 2013, by which time the family had decided to let everyone in on some of Frank's secrets. "I remember him saying things like, 'One day, they'll make it to where small distilleries can get back into business,'" Del says. "He was very firm in his belief. They would make the permitting process more feasible, to allow a small distillery to get into business.

"He knew how to make everything," Del says. "He had little tips and tidbits and secrets and recipes for just about anything you could think up. So we said, 'Heck, we'd be crazy not to go ahead and at least share some of this and share the story that he had.' It's truly a part of Charlotte history."

The first offerings from Seven Jars were vodka and a rum made with blackstrap molasses in a six-hundred-gallon hybrid pot and a copper column still. The distillery is currently aging bourbon in large charred oak barrels, but that won't be ready for a few years. In the meantime, using sourced spirits, it will release its Preamble Rye and Preamble Bourbon.

Seven Jars has plans for an apple pie whiskey—not to be confused with apple pie moonshine—based on the bourbon mash bill, as well as pickle-flavored and cherry-lemon vodkas and banana, pineapple, and dark rums.

"Personally," says Del, "we are all real traditionalists when it comes to aging bourbon, but there are some things you can do with it to get a good product. We're tweaking some of these things to try to stay as true as we can to the recipes and the methods they used but still be able to do it in a commercial production manner. We're focusing on the quality of the product and making sure we stay true to the art of what we're trying to do.

"You started to hear about these little distilleries popping up here and there. We were just kind of sitting here just watching it, and I was just in fascination, thinking, *Wow, I can't imagine that, fifty years before it happened, he* [Frank] *envisioned all of this.* I'm just tickled to death that we're doing what we're doing."

Del says the distillery is committed to using North Carolina products but concedes it will take some time to establish a consistent network. "Everything from the grains to the molasses," he says. That's the plan.

He says his father "loved anything that had to do with alcohol" and remembers Frank's making wine with locally grown muscadines and scuppernongs. "Any kind of grape that was grown, we made wine out of it."

Those jars . . . well, they held more than recipes. The totality of the contents, however, will apparently remain buried deep in family history. Says Del, "We don't talk about all the stuff that was in the jars."

Dragon Moonshine Company

516 East Fifteenth Street, Suite 14B
Charlotte, NC 28206
dragonmoonshine.com
Check the website to learn if tours and
tastings are available.

CHRIS WAGNER AND RICK LAVIN, both between jobs in their chosen fields, sold cars in Rochester, New York. It's where they met, about twenty-three years ago, and it's where they formed a lasting friendship. The men wound their way south, eventually settling in Charlotte.

Charlotte is where they talked about starting a business, where they grabbed some table napkins and started jotting ideas. Something recession-proof. Something they enjoyed.

Lavin, an experienced project manager, is a former army helicopter pilot. During flight school, he bunked with, as Wagner calls them, "spirits aficionados." Guys who knew a thing or two about making liquor. Lavin was intrigued. He developed an interest that has never waned.

The partners watched the birth and growth of North Carolina's micro-distilleries and noticed the loosening of time-worn laws. They got a license to produce alternative fuels, which allowed them to buy a small still—twenty-six gallons with a four-inch column. Lavin and Wagner wondered if they could make drinkable liquor, so they got to work.

Those cocktail napkins, those notes scribbled on scrap paper, became the foundation for Dragon Moonshine Company, which operates out of a seventeen-hundred-square-foot space in the artsy, beer-thirsty North Davidson, or NoDa, neighborhood of the Queen City.

"We're in phase one," says Wagner, who has a background in banking. "We like to call that 'one step out of the woods.'"

For now, Dragon is producing a moonshine and a silver rum in a pair of two-hundred-gallon hybrid column stills. The whiskey mash bill is

Dragon Moonshine Company produces moonshine and rum in a pair of two-hundred-gallon hybrid column stills.
Photo courtesy of Dragon Moonshine Company

composed of 70 percent corn, 20 percent barley, and 10 percent rye. The distillers use corn grits, in part because of the large surface area, which imparts more flavor from the grain.

The 80-proof rum begins with a wash consisting of brown sugar and molasses. "It seems to give us a really nice Caribbean feel to our silver rum," Wagner says of the distillation process. The distillers take a conservative approach to the foreshots and heads, striving for the greatest possible level of purity, even if that means trashing what other distillers might deem acceptable. "I'm in my forties," says Wagner, "and I'm tired of having a hangover."

The distillery, which obtained its license in 2014, is experimenting with a variety of aging methods for both of its products, including oak spirals, planks, and chips. Dragon also plans spiced and "navy-strength" versions of the rum, the latter bottled at between 110 and 114 proof.

The partners are completely self-funded, so product releases are staggered. "With what we make and what we want to bring out, it's cost-prohibitive to do more than one at a time," Wagner says. Dragon is trying to establish the rum in the ABC system and, in turn, develop cash flow to buy oak barrels. "If I've got to buy them one at a time, I'm going to do that and start putting rum and whiskey away," he says.

The partners plan to offer tours and tastings.

"Everything you see in our shop is repurposed for something else," Wagner says. The distillery ferments its mash in thousand-liter totes. The water is double-filtered, and a specially purposed tank recirculates the cooling water.

All dreamed up on napkins and loose sheets of paper.

"Let's see if we can make this work," says Wagner, paraphrasing the early conversations. They knew they could. The dragon and its invincible spirit, says Wagner, "have been symbols of strength throughout our lives, especially when things weren't going as planned."

He says, "When you come in and see the place, that's the type of atmosphere you get at this point. We're not like a vacation destination for distillers, or someone who wants to sit down in a café and sip on a whiskey from a Glencairn glass. Even though we have the Glencairn glasses, it's really something where we're putting everything we can into the quality of the product, not necessarily our surroundings."

Lavin and Wagner are talking with neighborhood brewers about using beer mash for distillation, as do Mother Earth Spirits in Kinston and Great Wagon Road Distilling Company, which is just across Charlotte.

Wagner, for the time being, is happy to admire the pristine German-made Kothe still of Ollie Mulligan of Great Wagon Road. "We were drooling over it the other day, looking at it from outside, because the door was locked. You probably see our face prints and handprints from where we were pressing our noses up on the glass."

All in good time.

Southern Grace Distilleries

NC 73 and Dutch Road
Mount Pleasant, NC 28124
southerngracedistilleries.com
704-622-6413
Visit the website to book a tour.

Leanne Powell gets out of the sleek, late-model Chevy Camaro, the latest design of the iconic muscle car. She leaves it in a barren parking lot at 1455 Dutch Road in Mount Pleasant.

She's dressed all in black, her long skirt and T-shirt bearing a white-on-black image and letters that read, simply, "Cash."

The shirt doesn't refer to money but rather pays homage to the music legend, "the Man in Black." Hindsight being what it is, black probably isn't the best choice on this searing hot June day. Yet it's somehow appropriate.

Powell's long blond bangs are dampened with sweat. She brushes them back, unfazed by the heat, which seems to intensify as it soaks into the bleak concrete and aging brick. No matter. Powell is downright enthusiastic.

"They showed us this, and we fell in love. We thought it was perfect."

It is a prison, the former Cabarrus County Correctional Center, which dates to the late 1920s and housed prisoners until 2011, when, holding fewer than two hundred inmates, it closed for good. Soldiers from Fort Bragg near Fayetteville used the closed prison for Robin Sage, an exercise in unconventional warfare and the final hurdle for candidates looking to become part of the army's elite Special Forces. It's dank and dismal—unkept grass, austere guard towers, overgrowth, as if it's the site of an episode of *Life After People*.

Never mind, Powell intimates. The scene is temporary, a blank canvas for what will be an extraordinary work of art.

Powell is the president of Southern Grace Distilleries, which makes Sun Dog 130, an uncut North Carolina moonshine—or, as she likes to call it, corn whiskey. Before the prison, the distillery was housed in a 2,200-square-

Southern Grace Distilleries has moved into the former Cabarrus County Correctional Center, which dates to the late 1920s and held prisoners until 2011.
Photo by NCDA&CS

foot space, part of a historic textile mill in Concord. It had been awhile since Mount Pleasant—a once-thriving textile community and home to the Lutheran-rooted Western Carolina Male Academy and Mont Amoena Seminary for women—saw significant economic development. The town, though, does have Marvin's Fresh Farmhouse restaurant, which showcases products grown and raised in North Carolina. A real-estate investment company bought the prison property. The agreement, says Powell, gives Southern Grace an option to buy in the coming years. The prison—which includes nineteen structures comprising 36,332 square feet, according to a posting by the state—encompasses 22.5 acres. The distillery plans to use less than a third of that.

"When I saw it, I remembered going to Buffalo Trace," says Powell, referring to the distillery in Frankfort, Kentucky. She talks about how that bourbon distillery uses different buildings for different products and mash bills. "You may have a white roof on one. One may be a terra-cotta building. One may be a wooden building." Referring to the constituent parts of her own operation, she says, "It will get hot, it will get cold, it will do just what we need to do to bring the product to maturity." Concrete walls and ceilings. Lots of space and plenty of water.

In Southern Grace's plans, barrels will be stacked high in a former mess hall, whiskey will be made in a newer dorm space—appropriately, cell block D—and merchandise will fill cells once used to separate especially troublesome prisoners. Visitors will look through windows, watching as the mash ferments. They'll walk into an original cell and rest their elbows on one of the few tasting bars inside a former prison. "It's very conducive to tourism," she says.

It's still a bit tough to imagine, to grasp. Memos for prisoners hang on the walls. A sign in a kitchen says, "Goodbye and have a healthy day."

Powell says she daydreams about taking a telescope to a watch tower and staring at the stars. But for now, her thoughts are more earthly, her vision focusing on the old prison. "This will be a nice big change for us."

A guard tower in the yard of the old prison
Photo by NCDA&CS

She talks about the swaths of empty space, which will become places to store and to bottle. The old distillery had little space for bonded storage—about a pallet's worth. "It's just a tiny little closet. Where we were was wonderful as an incubator site. We started off very quickly."

The idea for a distillery emerged in December 2013. By March 2014, Southern Grace had a building. Licenses were submitted by June 30 and finalized by the federal government on September 8. "We were on the shelves in February 2015."

Powell was chief of staff for Congressman Larry Kissell, a Democrat who represented North Carolina's Eighth District from 2009 until 2013. Partner and head distiller Tom Thacker, a former newspaper editor, worked for Kissell as well.

Powell says she began in politics as an intern in 1984 and by 1988 had a full-time job among lawmakers. "My whole life, I've spent time working with people where I talked about 'made in America, made in America, made in America.' I'd always wanted to find some way to manufacture something, to bring back jobs, that sort of thing."

Kissell, a graduate of Wake Forest University, lost to Republican Richard Hudson in 2012.

Powell and Thacker, close friends, talked about their respective futures. She had suffered a personal loss, and he had lost Mia, the dog whose portrait adorns the Sun Dog label.

"What do you really want to do?" she asked.

"I want to make liquor," Powell recalls Thacker saying.

"Okay, we're going to make liquor."

"I knew nothing about what to do," Powell says, "but I figured out a lot of it was dealing with the government and filling out paperwork and staying on top of stuff and doing marketing. Those were things I knew how to do."

A third partner brought his father's rye recipe, and it started there.

The Sun Dog recipe is 88 percent corn—sourced from North Carolina—and 12 percent barley.

"Tom has a much more sophisticated palate than I do, and he likes the ryes," Powell says. "He likes the spicier tastes. I have a very pedestrian palate, and this is what suited my palate. It comes off smooth to him, so he's happy with it. I think putting that barley in it smooths it out for the average consumer."

Southern Grace has been approved to make five products—pineapple, pink lemonade, and caramel apple "corn whiskeys" are planned, for example—which is one reason to expand. The barrels have to live somewhere, too.

"We've done one test barrel that's been up a little over a year now. At nine months, I was proud of it," Powell says. "We want to do a straight one as well. Our test barrel is a ten-gallon. We're going to the ten-gallon barrels for the stuff we're going to release earlier, and then we're doing fifty-three gallons for the straight. It will sit two, three years, whenever it's ready."

All from a copper still—fitted, says Powell, with "a tin man's hat"—fabricated in Cabarrus County. The distillery's thumb kegs originate in Asheville. "It's very old-fashioned, like what you might find in somebody's barn."

In a beautiful bit of irony, Powell suggests a walk to the chapel for a tasting. Rocks crunch under her feet, and she stops to show off a shell casing. The chapel, built in the 1990s, is quaint and simple. It's unadorned except for an ornate stained-glass window behind the pulpit.

She pops the cork on a brand-new bottle of 130-proof Sun Dog.

"Something that was important to me when we started this, we give money to charity for every bottle we sell. It's animal shelters for this, and we do a contest where people vote for which animal shelter in North Carolina the funds go to. We'll be doing the same thing in South Carolina."

Proceeds from the forthcoming products will go toward breast cancer research, for example.

"I came from a very high-pressure job. Most days, this is getting licked by kittens, compared to that. It's a job where we can make people happy. If we're doing a good job and we're selling a lot, we're helping a lot of dogs at an animal shelter, and hopefully people are enjoying our product responsibly and having a good time. The better we do, the more people we'll be able to hire and create jobs."

In talking with ABC officials and managers, the distillers learned that people were looking for a high-proof moonshine, far beyond the familiar 80 or 90 proof.

"We set out to do this," Powell says. "The reason most people won't do it is because the taxes are so high. When this bottle leaves my shop, I pay the federal government $3.26. It's a much higher federal excise tax when you're doing something this high in proof.

"I live for an old man in overalls to take that bottle, shake it up, turn it upside down, and be, like, 'I'll be damned.'

"When it passes an old-timer doing a proof test, I am happy."

Optimism Reigns in Statesville and Elsewhere

A glance at the North Carolina ABC Commission website shows about sixty active permits to distill spirits. Many of these are for operations with products listed on the commission's quarterly price list, on which this book is based. Some are wineries that have the intention to make brandy or fortified wines at some point. Some, such as Barrister & Brewer, which makes the popular Mystic Bourbon, are in the process of transitioning from contract arrangements to opening their own distilleries. B & B is building in Durham.

Others soon to come online include Bogue Sound Distillery in the community of Bogue, Kitty Hawk Stills in Greenville, and Elevated Mountain Distilling Company in Maggie Valley among several others.

Keeping track of new craft distilleries in the Old North State is like trying to dig a hole on a sandy beach. Expectant distillers in North Carolina are waiting on labels or other permits. They're waiting for distilling equipment or for barrels to fill. Whether the growth of distilleries continues at the current pace will depend largely on state lawmakers, customers' tastes, and, of course, product quality.

Southern Distilling Company in Statesville offers a grand example of optimism. Few areas have played a more colorful role in the state's liquor history than Iredell County and Statesville. Vienna and Pete Barger want a piece of that history. Their vision of their own distillery includes whiskey pouring from continuous columns and aging in oak barrels stacked high in a 25,000-square-foot building on 20 acres off I-77. The Bargers see two or three rickhouses as part of the distillery, which—set to open in 2017—will employ a 2,000-gallon cooker and a continuous column still from Vendome Copper & Brass Works in Louisville, Kentucky. Four 4,000-gallon fermenters will handle the initial runs; plans call for five more fermenters.

A wheated bourbon, says Pete, will be the core product. "We'll be doing a rye whiskey as well, but like anybody else who's starting in this business who plans to make an aged product, we have to do something to create revenue between today and when we actually can release that aged product. We'll be releasing some other products."

But no moonshine.

"We feel like we've got to focus on our core product, which is primarily bourbon, secondarily other whiskeys. But you've got to make ends meet in the meantime, so we will be doing some other things. But even those other things, a larger portion of that will be whiskeys."

Visitors to the new distillery will enter a large front room, where staff will greet them for tours, which will end, of course, at the tasting bar, positioned along a brick wall. It's where people will shop, where they'll be able to peer through large windows into the distillery, which will pump out fifteen hundred barrels the first year and increase to more than six thousand barrels of bourbon per year as the distillery ramps up to three shifts and continuous operation.

"We have capacity for much more," Vienna says. "All of the infrastructure relative to the boiler, chiller, cooling tower, etc., can support a second production facility just like this one on the other side of the plant and the eleven thousand square feet that's unfinished."

Customers can expect a five- or six-year-old bourbon, she says, which will age in fifty-three-gallon number-four char barrels. The rye will go in smaller barrels and will probably be ready after a couple of years.

The Bargers, who own a seventy-acre farm in northern Iredell County, briefly contemplated opening a winery. They talked about a plethora of business opportunities, but talk ended with the distillery.

"The idea actually originated from several years of really wanting to start a family business and establish our own business, and exploring lots of different opportunities and vetting lots of opportunities that came our way," Vienna says.

The Bargers thought about building the distillery on the farm, in a space that once held a barn, now fallen. It would have encompassed about three thousand square feet. But after much research and discussion with others in the industry, they decided they would have to go bigger, to focus on scale.

"One of the things that's important to people is that the product must be consistent, and that is one of the things that folks in the craft industry are really challenged with," Pete says.

Variables. A small change in the process can bring a big change in the result.

"A lot of our process, and a lot of time we spent developing our process and our plant, has been to do this in a way that allows us to be consistent, be efficient," he says. "The other thing that makes our plant unique is it's really on a very different scale than anybody else in the region. Unless somebody comes up in the area and surprises me in the future, we'll be the largest whiskey distillery outside Tennessee and Kentucky. When we are up and rolling, we will run that system three shifts a day, we will produce twelve thousand gallons of beer a day, and we will produce thirty-six and forty barrels of product a day. We won't start out that way. We'll have to build into that, and it will take time to get there, but that's the goal."

The distillery will initially offer heritage eight- and twelve-year bourbons—sourced from friends in the industry, Pete says—so it will have a product when it opens. The whiskey will be finished, blended, and bottled to create a flavor profile specific to Southern Distilling and unique in the industry.

"It takes a long time to build a proper distillery, so there's just a lot of moving parts and pieces that you wouldn't have in any other business," he says. "It's more highly regulated, probably, than anything outside pharmaceuticals, and maybe more so than pharmaceuticals when you consider how many local, state, and federal agencies are involved. There are a lot of people to get on board and a lot of technical challenges, but we're kind of on the downhill sprint right now, so we're feeling pretty good about things."

The distillery's Ashton Glover says Southern Distilling will make the first legal liquor in Iredell County since 1903. "We're excited to bring that whole industry back to this area," she says, "because it was a huge, driving force for the economy before it went away."

Call Family Distillers

1611 Industrial Drive
Wilkesboro, NC 28697
www.callfamilydistillers.com
336-990-0708
Visit the website to book a tour.

BRIAN CALL IS POINTING TO A BIG CAROLINA BLUE CHRYSLER, a Golden Lion edition. This one is fitted with toggle switches that kill the brake lights. That feature didn't come from the factory.

"It's my dad's favorite whiskey car," Call says, referring to his father, the legendary Willie Clay Call, a contemporary and friend of Junior Johnson, the Hall of Fame NASCAR owner and driver who spent time in prison for running illegal liquor.

Now on display at Call Family Distillers in Wilkesboro, the behemoth of an automobile once tore through the back roads of Wilkes and surrounding counties at the speed of white lightnin', all the while loaded down with some 130 jugs of crystal-clear moonshine. Brian pauses to demonstrate how distillers stored the filled jugs with the handles meeting in the center, which allowed strong 'shiners to hoist four containers at once.

Today, the Calls make perfectly legal sour mash moonshine.

"It's the same recipe my dad taught me," Brian says of the Wilkes County distillery's line of 'shine, made with white cornmeal—ground the old-timey way in a mill just down the road—barley malt, wheat, and cane sugar.

They're called "craft" distilleries for a reason, a designation that starts with locally grown products and culminates at a usually "modest" bottling station, says Brad Call, Brian's nephew and the distillery's COO. The big distillers in Tennessee and Kentucky—those that run liquor twenty-four hours a day, thirteen days at a time to keep up with demand—fill hundreds of bottles each minute. The Calls bottle four large Mason jars at a time, which is typical for distillers on the North Carolina trail.

The Calls use individually quick-frozen fruits to infuse a strawberry

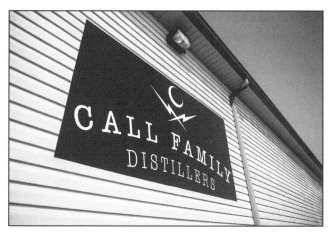

Call Family Distillers makes its line of moonshine in Wilkesboro.
Photo courtesy of Call Family Distillers

moonshine, a cherry moonshine, and an apple pie moonshine, which, Brian says, is probably their bestseller.

Willie Clay Call learned to make liquor from his father, Willie Simon Call, who was simply carrying on the family business. In Appalachia, people far removed from cities and their relatively abundant resources made moonshine as a matter of tradition. But making the highly profitable white liquor was also a means to feed themselves and their families. Whiskey entrepreneurs still make liquor in the woods, mostly to avoid taxes but partly to honor the past. In Wilkes County, Holly Farms pulled some moonshiners out of the woods and off the roads when the poultry company opened a plant in Wilkesboro in the late 1950s. Some moonshiners, says Brad, probably used the factory experience to their benefit.

The product goes by many names—white lightning, white whiskey, corn liquor, white dog, and moonshine among them. Recipes often include corn as the main ingredient but may also call for varying amounts of wheat, malted barley, sugar, rye, and yeast. The distilled white liquor can then serve as a base for fruit liquors and whiskeys such as bourbon.

The Calls' white liquor comes off the still about 150 proof, or 75 percent alcohol. They employ reverse osmosis to deionize the water, which they use to lower the proof. "We bring it down to 101, where you can drink it," Brian says.

The Calls ferment the grain mash in thousand-pound barrels, which they make at the distillery using clear white pine "from just across the river," says Brad. The Calls and Copper Barrel Distillery, located about four miles east on the north side of the Yadkin River, heat the mash using uniquely distinct—and proprietary—methods of steam injection.

As Brian walks through the distillery—an open warehouse-type space with plenty of room to expand—he points toward a five-hundred-gallon copper pot. It's immediately obvious this huge pot—now beaten, slashed, and tucked away in a dark corner—produced more than a few good gulps of whiskey in its time. "The revenuers chopped that thing up years ago," Brian says. The ax marks, mostly on the bottom of the pot, are still deep, jagged.

Brian designed the Calls' shiny new still, built by Vendome Copper & Brass Works, a prominent still maker that counts Jim Beam among its many customers. In stark contrast to big whiskey makers such as Beam, the Calls hauled the still back to North Carolina from Louisville with a twenty-eight-foot trailer pulled by a pickup. Brian refers to the still as a mix of new school and old.

Indeed.

For the Calls of Wilkes County, distilling moonshine is a tradition spanning seven generations, at least as far back as the Reverend Daniel Call, who, because of pressure from his congregation, sold his still—seven generations ago—to whiskey enthusiast and burgeoning entrepreneur Jack Daniel.

Photos of moonshiners and revenuers greet visitors to the distillery. The shelves and floor are decorated with mash barrels and grand copper stills—complete with bullet holes—along with axes and sledgehammers and rustic tools used to shell corn and make cornmeal.

The Calls' steam-injection still occupies a good portion of an open warehouse-sized space at the distillery. In the same space, a few dozen yards away, sit a sterling 1940 Ford and the 1961 Chrysler still used for promotional events and bottle signings. People gather nearby to hear stories, to tell stories, and to relive the history of the surrounding Blue Ridge Mountains—to learn about the place the Calls know as "the Moonshine Capital of the World."

Brad tells of how Willie Clay Call would drive to local malls, where he talked to people about the history and culture of moonshine. He talked about a time when, before NASCAR expanded westward, stock-car pioneers descended from moonshiners ran laps around the defunct and decaying short track that was once the revered North Wilkesboro Speedway. Willie Clay Call wanted to preserve a history crafted with corn, water, patience, and fortitude, regardless of whether liquor was made in a fireproof building or under a forest canopy.

Brian Call designed the Calls' still, built by Vendome Copper & Brass Works of Kentucky.
Photo by Lisa Snedeker

"It's the notion that whoever made it was not paying a tax on it," Brad says of the romanticism that surrounds illegal moonshining. "If anything, we feel like there's a sense—more so now, pride—in reference to us being here doing this legally. Wilkes County has always had that notion of moonshine and being proud of it at the heart, but being out and telling someone that this is a place that was very well known. That wasn't something that Wilkes Countians could really do up until now.

"People can argue the usage of the word *moonshine*, and the semantics of what that may mean—this, that, and the other—but ultimately, I guess, what it does come down to is there's a distiller that's making this product, whether it's in the woods or underneath the roof in a building, where they're paying the taxes. Someone like Brian, who's been taught from one of the most famous moonshiners. He carries that expertise whether he's making it outside or inside, whether he's paying a tax on it or not. If he made this same product and didn't pay a tax on it, it would still taste the same. It would be the same quality as if he was paying the tax on it."

The Calls, Brian says, use food-grade equipment in a spotless facility. "That's the difference I see," he says. "You ain't pullin' no damned possum out

The Calls ferment their grain mash in barrels that hold a thousand pounds, which they make at the distillery from clear white pine.
Photo courtesy of Call Family Distillers

of your mash barrel, a squirrel or something that's got in there."

Willie Clay Call was never caught making or running moonshine, although he did serve time on a so-called conspiracy charge, Brian says of his father. "At one time in Wilkes County, Dad says you got a still up, and if the still stayed a month, you were doing good. There were so many revenue officers walking the creeks and springs finding stills. He said it got so hot one time, he went Down East and worked a little while. It wasn't worth your time putting a still up 'cause the revenuer would be on it in two or three weeks."

Oh, how things have changed.

The Calls say the law allowing on-site sales has certainly helped their business, which also gets a boost each year in April during MerleFest, an annual Americana music festival founded by Doc Watson to honor his son Merle, who died in a farming accident. The distillery is just steps from the festival's primary campground.

Says Brian, "The reason we even went with moonshine is because of my family history. A lot of people, they just decide they want to make a moonshine, and they ain't got no history."

Copper Barrel Distillery

508 Main Street
North Wilkesboro, NC 28659
copperbarrel.com
336-262-6500
Visit the website to book a tour.

THE TASTING BAR AT COPPER BARREL DISTILLERY is underneath a pair of heavy metal doors, the entrance to the boiler of the old Key City Furniture factory in North Wilkesboro. The factory closed in 2013.

"That's where the maintenance crew used to have to climb inside the boiler, scrub it out, and inspect it," says George Smith as he looks up at the doors.

Smith is the founder and CEO of Copper Barrel, which has occupied the old factory since the spring of 2015. Some of the building's original bricks, thanks to Smith, remain.

As he pours his white whiskey, Smith talks about the recipes and the business. He talks of Buck Nance, his master distiller. Nance's father invented the type of steam-distillation process Smith now employs, he says. Now past seventy, Nance has distilled liquor for sixty years, all the while perfecting his recipes, among them a white-lightning moonshine and fruit liquors including strawberry, blueberry, black cherry, and red cherry.

Infusing white whiskey with blueberries, for instance, seems a bit unconventional. Nope, Smith says. "That was purposeful. We wanted to have flavors that are unique. You really get to enjoy the flavor of the fruit."

They're Nance's bestsellers. Historically speaking, of course.

"It's the same way Buck has done it," which includes going easy on the sugar, says Smith. "We throw the rye, the corn, the cane sugar into the mash, add the water and yeast. So it's five ingredients. That's it."

There's much more to the story, of course. And to be fair, the recipe probably isn't exactly the same.

Nance refers to himself as a perfectionist. He doesn't vary from the time-honored handed-down mash bill. Yet he tinkers with different grains, mash bills, flavors. "If it's out there, I will play with it," he says.

George Smith and Buck
Nance make a variety of
moonshine flavors in their
North Wilkesboro distillery.
Photo by Lisa Snedeker

That process led him to the 'shine he and Smith share with the world. "I played with it, got it to where I wanted it, to where I thought it was a good drink. I played with it over a period of years 'til I got it to where I thought it was almost a perfect drink. I still fool with the recipe a little bit here and there."

Nance doesn't drink much alcohol. But that's not to say he doesn't drink at all. "I want a good, smooth drink when I do drink," he says. "I don't want something that sets you on fire, or something with an aftertaste. I just want a good, true, authentic moonshine. Some of the stuff out here on the market, it's not drinkable. It's not good."

Nance is a local legend. Smith, however, came to North Carolina from Vermont, where, growing up, he spent time on a farm. Work, including a tenure with IBM, brought him to Charlotte, where he eventually became president of a local bourbon club and met Bill Samuels Jr. of Maker's Mark.

Smith told Samuels he was thinking about opening a distillery.

Really? Samuels asked.

"I said, 'Yeah, actually, I really am.'

"He said, 'I tell you what. I'll give you my cell-phone number, and if you have a couple of friends interested in going into business with you, give me a call, and I'll introduce you to everyone you need to know in the industry to get started off on the right foot.'"

Smith and a friend had talked about opening a microbrewery. North Carolina had too many of those already, they decided. They both liked whis-

George Smith is the founder and CEO of Copper Barrel Distillery, which has occupied the Key City Furniture factory since the spring of 2015.
Photo by Lisa Snedeker

key better anyway. Smith remembers telling the friend. "'Let's figure out how to make whiskey.' I said, 'I'll give Bill a call. I don't know what he's going to say. The worst thing he's going to say is he's too busy.' I called Bill, and the next thing I knew, we had a trip to Kentucky planned. When I got back, I told my friends, 'Guys, I'm going to do this, with or without you.'"

Smith made a list of criteria—access to fresh water, local grains, demographics related to tourism, those sorts of things—and visited some twenty cities in North Carolina before choosing North Wilkesboro, where he met Nance, who planned to help Smith install the equipment and teach him to use it. The men became friends.

"He came to me one day and said, 'George, I don't know if you're interested, but I think I'd like to work with you full-time.' I was shocked," Smith says. "It's been amazing working with this guy, getting to know him and hear his stories. He's got it down to a science. I couldn't have paid for that type of knowledge and experience."

The distillery, says Smith, uses the only licensed and operating well within the city limits, a crystalline rock aquifer. Its whiskey is the product of equipment that Nance, with the help of a local welder, designed and built. "Even those copper coils, which look like they're machine-rolled, Buck did that by hand, bending it over his knee."

Smith says, "Our product is truly authentic—from the grain to the water to everything. This is why, I believe, Buck decided he wanted to partner with me. He realized very quickly that we both have a strong regard for integrity.

"We make every drop from scratch on-site here. Smith says Copper

Barrel moonshine "really falls into the specialty category, because it's a mix of both cane and grain. I think that's what makes it a unique product."

Smith walks toward the steam-injection still, where, he says, "the magic happens." He points to the large cooling tank, which holds 250 long copper coils, a serpentine work of art visible only from the last steps on a folding ladder.

The white lightning comes out around 140 proof, and it's bottled around 96. For its flavored liquors, Copper Barrel soaks the fruit in the white whiskey for thirty to sixty days, extracting its intense flavor.

The process regarding the fruit was key. Smith knew that. But as for the types of fruit, well, he wasn't so sure. "I debated even myself, originally, when Buck said we needed to do a red cherry and a black cherry. I'm, like, 'Why do we need to do both?'"

Buck told him. Not everyone likes black cherries; not everybody likes red cherries. The flavors are distinct. Separate. Red cherries are tart. Black cherries, which contain more natural sugar, are sweeter.

At the tasting bar, under those heavy metal doors, Smith—working one at a time—poured all of his products into small, clear plastic cups. This was moonshine, made from long-held recipes. Some flavors were new, experimental, not yet ready for market—the espresso, green apple, and crème brûlée, for example.

Nance wasn't thrilled with the new flavors. At least not right away.

"I told him, 'Buck, I completely agree. We gotta start with your products. However, the younger generation, they like more unique flavors.'"

Nance told Smith to do it.

Smith did. He came up with six flavors. People tried them. They liked them. Nance liked them. "He's, like, 'George, those flavors are pretty good. I see the people's reaction, and it's gonna sell.'"

In a way, Copper Barrel stands as a tribute to Wilkes County and its history of fine 'shine. In fact, "Wilkes County NC" is imprinted in raised letters on the bottle. Every bottle.

"This is a true 'shine that people can remember from years back," Nance said in an interview that is part of a video posted on the distillery's Facebook page. "People in this area who drink moonshine, they know moonshine. There's more good moonshine made right here in this county than anywhere else in the world."

Mayberry Spirits Distillery

461 North South Street
Mount Airy, NC 27030
facebook.com/mayberryspirits
336-719-6860
Tours are offered at the top of the hour
   from noon to 5 P.M. on Friday and every
   half-hour from noon to 5:30 P.M. on
   Saturday.

PEOPLE COME TO MOUNT AIRY—MAYBERRY, if you prefer—to peek into an idealized past. It's a place where Barney Fife is made immortal via clocks and cardboard cutouts. Where Andy and Opie, fishing poles in hand, are always headed to the lake. Where Aunt Bee still makes pies, jams, and jellies.

Barney still bumbles, and Otis still stumbles.

"We have a little more of a tour experience than most places do," Vann McCoy of Mayberry Spirits Distillery says. "We designed our company to include this because it's Mayberry, and we wanted a fun experience for people."

Labels on the distillery's products—"RFD" means "Really Fine Drink"—play on the Mayberry theme. As tourists leave, McCoy thanks them for visiting his "Really Fine Distillery" and wishes them a "Really Fine Day."

Visitors entering the distillery can't help seeing, stenciled on a far wall in large, prominent cursive, three unpretentious words that form a sentence both profound and eloquent: "Lift your spirit."

Sound and simple.

Mayberry Spirits makes a 100-proof handcrafted white whiskey called Crystal Moon, a hyper-aged Toasted Oak, and a Toasted Vanilla.

McCoy says, "When you age any kind of spirit, what you're really doing is creating a wood extract."

McCoy, who ages with toasted oak chips, wears many hats. Literally. He changes hats based on the subject as he guides visitors through his distillery.

As would an entertaining college professor, McCoy deftly leads them through the distilling process, explaining each detail with meticulous precision. He wears a white baker's hat while talking about extracts, a line of which he makes and sells as well.

"Extracts are made using a solvent and a base material. In this case, our solvent is our Crystal Moon. We put that alcohol in contact with American oak. The alcohol in contact with the oak will suck out the essential oils of oak, what we call tannins or tannic acid. It's that oil of oak that gives you your color and your flavor in any of your aged spirits. It's the amount of oil of oak that determines, in a sense, your aging. The difference is enormous."

After his freshman year in college, McCoy returned to Mount Airy in search of work. A temp service hired him to package socks in the basement of this same building on North South Street.

"I've gone from packaging warm and fuzzy things to making things that will make you warm and fuzzy." He chuckles.

The visitors chuckle.

"Oh, me," he says in a display of Mayberry charm.

McCoy was at a summer enrichment camp at Western Carolina University when he got the idea to make whiskey. He learned about Appalachian culture—recipes, bluegrass, playing the dulcimer, moonshining, things like that.

He was thirteen.

McCoy thought about moonshine. About making it. *Doesn't look that hard*, he told himself. So he got to work.

"I found some cornmeal under the cupboard, and I found some bread yeast in the other cupboard, and mixed it all up with some sugar, and put it on the back porch. About a week later, my mom comes home, walks in the door, and her pressure cooker is on the stove with some copper pipe puttied to it going over into the kitchen sink. My condenser."

She asked what he was doing.

McCoy stayed quiet.

Was he making liquor?

McCoy nodded.

She laughed. Out loud.

"She says, 'Well, I hadn't told you, but I guess it's time. Your family's been making it around here and running it for about 150 years, and you just can't help it, can you? It must be in your blood.'"

At sixteen, he went off to study astrophysics. But God had other plans, he says. "The Big G," McCoy calls him.

"I ended up being a contemplative monk for twenty-five years in Swit-

Vann McCoy, founder of Mayberry Spirits Distillery, wears many hats.
Photo by Lisa Snedeker

zerland, Ireland, Minnesota, and Wisconsin. I did the Gregorian chant thing. My mother's health started declining, so I moved back three years ago to honor thy mother. I'm the only relative."

McCoy needed something to do upon returning home. He noticed how the wine industry had exploded in North Carolina, particularly in the nearby Yadkin Valley. Breweries, too, were popular and emerging. *Distilling is next,* he thought.

"We thought it would take us six to eight months to get it going. It ended up taking three years, with all the regulations and hoops to go through. They thought we were going to blow up Mayberry. It was all kinds of things. It required us to wear many hats in pulling all of this together."

He grabs one—a worn and beaten straw hat with a wide brim, his "yeast-wrangling hat."

Yeast and sugar make alcohol, McCoy says. "When you're starting out to make alcohol, what you're looking for initially are sugars. Yeast and sugar make alcohol. That's the short version."

Sugars emanating from grains—corn, oats, rye, wheat, barley—make whiskey. Fruits—apples, peaches, pears, bananas, cherries—make brandy. Starchy vegetables—potatoes, sweet potatoes, pinto beans—produce vodka.

McCoy makes whiskey, although you'll taste neither corn nor rye, neither barley nor wheat. His whiskey is made with a syrup produced from gluten-free sorghum grain.

"The sorghum plant has two parts. It's a cane plant. It looks a little like corn or sugarcane. In that cane is a sweet juice, and that juice is what is heated up and rendered down to make molasses, just like sugarcane."

Molasses makes rum, he says. "We, on the other hand, are using the other part of the sorghum plant. So, at the top of the stalk of the cane is a grain tassel, a little like you see on corn. It's those grains that we're using to get the syrup. So it's coming from the grain world, which means the final product is technically a whiskey, but because the syrup is so close to both molasses and agave, our final clear product, or unaged product, is really closer in taste profile to a rum or a tequila."

It's a cross between honey and caramel, he explains. A rich, buttery texture. A pleasant sweetness.

"What we discovered when we did our initial distillations with this product was that the final product that came out, the spirits, were exceptionally smooth, and that was what surprised us. I had never heard of sorghum to start with, much less distilled with it."

McCoy learned about sorghum during an event celebrating traditional methods of farming. The event was held in the shadow of Pilot Mountain, which rises more than two thousand feet above the state park that bears its name. The peak is what remains of the Sauratown Mountains, a point of demarcation along US 52 as it winds through the wine-rich Yadkin Valley.

He watched artisans shuck corn and crush sorghum cane to extract the juices.

"They were cooking it over on the side, and I said, 'What is that?' I tasted it and said, 'Whew, I might be able to make something out of this.' We were going to make regular whiskeys at first, but we discovered this and said, 'Oh, my gosh.'"

A grand idea, as he puts it.

McCoy takes ten to fifteen gallons of that syrup and adds forty gallons of hot water, which he places in old Mt. Olive pickle barrels. He adds yeast. It is time, as his worn straw hat suggests, to wrangle the little buggers.

McCoy then turns historian, reflecting on a time when the only distilleries were hidden under canopies of pine and cherry trees. Maples and oaks.

"Those further out in the woods, who either couldn't afford bread yeast or were either too lazy or drunk to go home to get it, would have to resort to naturally occurring yeasts. And one of the best places to find those out in

Vann McCoy's whiskey is made with a sorghum syrup produced from gluten-free sorghum grain.
Photo by Lisa Snedeker

nature, believe it or not, is in cow patties. It's a warm, moist medium when it comes out, and it draws in natural atmospheric yeasts. So they would pitch cow patties into their mash, and it worked kinda so-so."

The patties produced low yields and some unsurprisingly funky tastes.

"What I want you to remember from this, however, is that here at Mayberry Spirits, we use only the finest commercial distilling yeast possible to get pure, clear, and awesome-tasting spirits. So that when you think Mayberry Spirits, you think, 'No shit.'"

Oh, me.

McCoy grabs a long, gray beard to hide his normally clean-shaven face. He's hiding from the revenuers, you see.

He uses two natural-gas-powered copper pot stills—a hundred gallons and five gallons—and reflux cones to make his base Crystal Moon.

McCoy dons a white lab coat and starts shaking a clear glass jar, presumably filled with whiskey. "Bubbles will appear in higher-proof alcohol much more quickly and pop much more quickly," he explains.

Pretty elementary, and the method available to those in the woods who couldn't afford a proofing hydrometer, which measure liquids' density. The faster the bubbles dissipate, the higher the proof.

Crystal Moon and Toasted Oak are bottled at 100 proof. The Toasted

Oak whiskey smells of caramel, honey, and molasses, with a hint of the oak. There's a subtle sweetness on the palate that builds toward a warm, unusually smooth finish. The 90-proof Toasted Vanilla—Toasted Oak blended with Madagascar vanilla—stands alone, says McCoy, as "a good sipping whiskey." Mix it if you will because, as McCoy points out, "vanilla goes with everything."

McCoy leads the group into the tasting room. He finds a fedora and flops it atop his head. Now, he's a bartender.

It all makes for an interesting dichotomy—the theatrics, props, and such juxtaposed with the handmade items and decorations hanging on the walls and lining the shelves throughout the homey reception area. All local and sustainable.

"We try to bring that artisan distilling into our retail area," he says. Hand-blown whiskey glasses, soaps, hand-rolled cigars infused with Toasted Vanilla, gourmet baking extracts, infused salts and sugars . . .

Some of the wood and tin on the walls comes from a barn built fifty years ago. The chandeliers were made from parts and pieces taken from the farm. The display cases were once the windows of the old farmhouse. The T-shirts are made locally from cotton grown in North Carolina. The walls pay homage to regional artists.

McCoy starts to pour drinks and begins talking about the Toasted Oak. "Unlike your corn- and rye- and barley-based whiskey, it doesn't have that kinda harsh, caustic after-catch you're used to. There's a smoothness to it that's unusual."

He reflects on the aging process, smiling as he thinks about the future of spirits. The possibilities.

"We are no longer tied to having a hardwood barrel," he says. "This means we're no longer restricted to oak as an aging agent, as an extract base. We can now go to other kinds of wood, softer wood—for example, apple or peach or hickory or mesquite or pecan or cherry. All these sorts of things are now possible because of the way we can do the aging—the inside-out way, if you will. That will be the next big movement in your craft distilling—alcohols of various kinds aged in different wood bases."

The show goes on.

Broad Branch Distillery

756 North Trade Street
Winston-Salem, NC 27101
broadbranchdistillery.com
336-602-2824
Tours and tastings are offered at 6:30 P.M.
on the first and third Friday of each
month.

FRANK WILLIAMS HELD THE JAR of dark, aged liquor. He studied it.

John Fragakis asked what was in the bottle.

Williams said he didn't know. Some kind of brown whiskey.

"He can't wait to take the cap off," says Fragakis, who is telling the story. "He looks like he's taking it off slow, but it's almost like a sleight of hand. Next thing you know, the cap's off and he's holding it and smelling it. He says, 'This stuff is good.' So he takes a swig out of the jar."

Aged whiskey. Williams knew that. Exactly what, he didn't know.

"Frank," said Fragakis, "it's your Nightlab."

Fragakis recalls, "He was just jumping for joy. I didn't want to obscure the flavors, because I thought it was going to be a delicate drink, but it turns out it's an awesome drink when it's aged."

Williams's recipe has been shared and passed on. Shared deep in the woods, on scraps of dog-eared paper.

Now in his late seventies, Williams started making liquor when he was a boy. Initially, family, friends, and acquaintances brought together Williams, Fragakis, and business partner Nick Doumas, who died in October 2016.

Whiskey solidified the relationship. Like family.

Broad Branch Distillery is on Trade Street on the northern edge of downtown Winston-Salem. The distillery is in a former tobacco warehouse, once part of an industry and a company, R. J. Reynolds, that still define this town, once nicknamed "Camel City." Growth and revitalization have taken hold. Broad Branch is smack-dab in an area bordered by the Innovation Quarter, an extension of Wake Forest University. It's in a section of the city

stocked with hip dive bars and creative bartenders, with trendy restaurants overseen by visionary chefs. Bands just this side of famous play Americana, rock, and bluegrass on outdoor stages and in shiny new parks dedicated to the arts.

To the uninformed or incurious, Broad Branch is a dichotomy, a clash of tradition and modernity. Yet it all makes sense.

Fragakis, who has decades of experience in wine and liquor distribution, prefers to start the story at the beginning. A distiller who wants to make good liquor should, like a great musician, first learn all the notes, get to the essence of the whiskey or the music.

Frank Williams's grandfather, born in the late 1800s, made whiskey from a still in Patrick County, Virginia. Williams's father also made whiskey. As Fragakis tells it, Frank, age seven, and his brother, eight, often helped their father with the mash. They were ready to hit the woods.

"Y'all go up there," Frank's father said. "I'll be up in a bit."

So they waited. And waited some more. Until they got tired of waiting.

"'We'll just make it ourselves,'" says Fragakis, slowly recounting the story.

The boys made the mash and were proud of it.

"This is stuff that comes off the kitchen table," Fragakis says. "They would eat it if they weren't making whiskey out of it."

What happened next was entirely predictable. Frank's father got mad. But the boys pleaded with him to try it. He did.

"'Okay,'" he told the boys, according to Fragakis. "'You two make it from now on.'"

The boys recovered an old still the family kept under the house.

Frank began distilling at twelve and by thirteen owned a car. He tried to become a legitimate distiller. Never worked out. In the 1980s, during the gas crunch, he got his wife a license to make ethanol.

"Frank tried really, really hard to go legitimate," says Fragakis. "He worked on it for four years, had the brand, had the label. He's known for making really, really good stuff. He's just wonky about distillation."

The way Williams figured, if he couldn't make a go of it with his grandfather's recipe, he would share it with someone who could. The distillery shipped its first product, the 91-proof unaged Nightlab, in the summer of

Broad Branch Distillery co-owner John Fragakis pours a taste at his distillery in Winston-Salem.
Photo by Lisa Snedeker

2015. Broad Branch mills its grains at the distillery in a sophisticated rolling mill that can grind nearly five thousand pounds in an hour.

"The first time we ground here, we knew we had the right thing because we had an explosion of aroma," Fragakis says.

Non-GMO white heirloom corn from Stanly County. Malted barley from Epiphany Craft Malt in Durham. Rye from an undisclosed farmer—even to the distillery—from the plains of western Washington. Louisiana sugar. East Kent Golding hops, imparting floral and citrus notes.

At the back of the distillery, a huge tank holds eighty-five hundred gallons of water from an artesian well in Surry County; the high calcium content helps stabilize the pH.

"Everything is larger than we need. I wish we were this large, but we're not," Fragakis says. "We have such ancient ways of wanting to do things, it takes us way longer. Is that going to be smart? If we survive, it's going to be smart as hell. If we don't make it . . ."

Fragakis fails to finish the thought.

Williams got a taste of the first product distilled by Broad Branch. As did Nancy Fraley, a professional "nose" and highly regarded distilling consultant. "When I give my partner a hug and smell her hair, I can pretty much tell what she's eaten the entire day," she told *The Atlantic* in April 2015. "Not that I go around smelling people's hair. But it definitely comes in handy for my job."

Says Fragakis, "She's an eclectic woman who has probably as keen a sense of smell for analyzing whiskey as anybody. We send off samples to her all the time. Matter of fact, she kind of guides us. We made our first batch five times before we got to the right place, sending samples back and forth, this direction, that direction. She tells us how good we are, then she sends us a whole paragraph of what we have to work on. She told us one time it was very, very good. I felt like little Johnny Fragakis in the first grade, with my short pants on, and I got my first gold star. I was beaming from ear to ear."

Regarding the early samples, Williams was impressed. Mostly.

"Congratulations, y'all. This is better than I can make," he told the distillers. But . . .

"You're heavy on the rye."

Hmm, Fragakis thought. "I said, 'Okay, Frank. We'll back off on the rye.'

"We get an email from Nancy, who had just gotten our sample."

She complimented Broad Branch on its good work.

But . . .

A little heavy on the rye.

"So," says Fragakis, "we have a guy from Alleghany County and a woman from Berkeley who flies all over the world, and they had the exact same analysis on this thing. Except for backing off on the rye, we haven't touched his recipe."

The distillery plans to introduce a 100 percent "killer" rye whiskey. And Fragakis says it is "making a whiskey mash and putting it in barrels to make bourbon. We're actually aging a North Carolina whiskey. And rum, too, using corn and molasses from Louisiana, from a family that's been farming for seven generations.

"This is kind of exciting and gives craft distillers some hope," says Fragakis, who in another time worked in the Caribbean, where he called on rum makers. "These large companies are locked into a style. They just can't say, 'Okay, we're changing our style.' We can, but they can't. We're into this grain- or ingredient-forward style, and they aren't."

Says distiller Joe Tappe, "You can do documentaries, you can do audiobooks. Ken Burns can do all his best." He may mean Burns's *Prohibition*, from 2011. "But under the tutelage of a guy who has been doing this since he was seven years old, there's no way to really experience history except by tasting what he's made."

Sutler's Spirit Co.

840 Mill Works Street
Winston-Salem, NC 27101
sutlersspiritco.com
336-565-6006
Call the distillery to book a tour.

Scot Sanborn heats the red wax and waits several seconds to be sure it has melted just enough for the stamp to leave a lasting impression, a reminder of his nascent business. He returns the booklet bearing the stamp to his guest on the other side of the bar. He repeats the act several more times for several more guests.

The stamping process captures Sanborn's personality and work ethic. It represents a passion for his work, his craft.

Sanborn owns Sutler's Spirit Co., a craft distillery nearly hidden in the shadows of an expansive building that's part of the once-gritty but now-trendy West End district on the edge of downtown Winston-Salem.

It's Saturday evening, and Sanborn has just finished guiding fifteen or so visitors on a tour.

Sutler's, named for the purveyors of alcohol and other goods who traveled with armies, makes small-batch gin and rum. The rum is aging—becoming darker and richer—in new and used charred white oak bourbon barrels stacked along a wall near the bar. Made with sugarcane syrup and molasses in a copper still crafted in Portugal, the rum, at this point in late 2016, is still waiting to hit the market.

The aging rum, already in the barrels for several months, has to be right. He'll release it when it's ready.

He's still waiting.

"My heart and soul's in it," says Sanborn, who began making liquor at home in his garage.

Visitors to Sutler's Spirit Co. enter through a side door off a side porch. To the right is a popular bar. Sutler's is to the left. Soft jazz plays from a

Scot Sanborn talks to a group of visitors about his distillery and its products, a gin and a rum that has yet to be released.
Photo by Lisa Snedeker

speaker set high in the corner of the candle-lit room. Moose the Golden-doodle is quick to greet visitors.

Sanborn is standing behind the tasting bar, which separates him from four barstools that are now empty. He's concentrating on a drinking glass. He wipes it clean and carefully lays it on the bar, alongside another just like it. He points at each glass and silently counts.

"It's a dream come true," he says.

A few minutes later, the place is filled for a fully booked tour.

Finding and securing a marketable name is an arduous process. It's one thing to come up with a name. It's a much bigger thing to secure a trademark, a process that can take weeks, months. Sanborn calls sutlers "traveling bar-tenders." The distillery's black ceramic bottles are made in Germany. The letters on the bottles are stenciled in old gold. Not coincidentally, the colors are like those of nearby Wake Forest University. Most prominent on the bottle is

Scot Sanborn owns Sutler's Spirit Co., a craft distillery in Winston-Salem's West End district.
Photo by Lisa Snedeker

the word *Gin*, printed in large letters, much as sutlers would have written it, so as to identify it among liquors in crates filled with identical bottles.

The bottles, Sanborn says, are difficult to work with because they're ceramic, and imperfections are inherent. But "liquor bottles in the old days were ceramic," he says. "We felt it complemented the brand. I liked the history, so I ran with it."

Sanborn hasn't stopped running. Metaphorically speaking, anyway. Handsome and friendly, he travels to events to promote his products and those of fellow distillers. He traverses the state to meet with local ABC boards, then returns home to his family, which includes a new daughter. He makes gin and rum and guides tours of his distillery.

A dozen or so people stand around the tasting bar, where—after the short history lesson—talk turns to spirits. Sanborn stops near a copper alembic still. The two interconnected vessels heat the wash, which boils at around 174 degrees Fahrenheit, and condense the vapors into alcohol. The design goes back centuries.

Sanborn uses a column—or reflux—still, which sits a few feet from the copper alembic, to produce his gin. The column still contains a series of plates, each working to condense the vapors again and again as they travel up the still. In the process, the gin retains more pure, clean alcohol.

Sanborn and distiller Tim Nolan—a bartender who also managed a bar next door—use a gin basket and eight fresh botanicals, including lavender, coriander, and juniper. The duo experimented with up to twenty-five botanicals. Getting it right took more than ten months.

"I taught him how to distill and realized he was highly passionate and had a better palate than me, so I let him be the mad scientist with the gin," Sanborn says. "We did not rush. We took our time. We made a lot of bad gin. We made a lot of good gin. Some experiments we might come back to.

"As long as you have the juniper berry, you can add any botanical from that point on—rose petals, grass clippings. As long as it doesn't cause cancer or is hallucinogenic, you can add it." Approval from the Food and Drug Administration is necessary, of course.

"I like bourbon, I like whiskey, and I like gin," Sanborn says. "When I started off the distillery, I knew I couldn't afford all the equipment to do a whiskey. I needed to make a product quickly, and gin is quick."

The word *quick* is relative. Sure, gin can be made relatively quickly. But finding the perfect combination of botanicals and correctly infusing them into the alcohol is a process as varied as it is difficult.

Eventually, you wing it, he says. You learn on your own.

In Sutler's Gin, the juniper is unmistakable, but it's mostly in the background. The citrus is more pronounced. The gin is so smooth that tonic becomes an afterthought. One ice cube and a splash of lemon work well.

"I wanted to make something I have a passion for," Sanborn says. "We're selling it as fast as we can make it."

Piedmont Distillers, Inc.

3960 US 220
Madison, NC 27025
piedmontdistillers.com
336-445-0055
Call for information about tours.

THE OLD TRAIN DEPOT ON THE EDGE OF DOWNTOWN MADISON is worn and forgotten, empty, its wooden façade faded by time and weather. Weeds jut from the parking lot. The grass around the building is long and weedy. Posted signs from Norfolk Southern promise prosecution for trespassers and dumpers.

No matter. There's nothing to see anyway. Not anymore. But it's where, in 2005, Piedmont Distillers produced the first legal liquor in North Carolina since Prohibition, in a former train station that's about the size of an average four-bedroom ranch-style suburban home. The distillery outgrew the old depot and in 2012 moved across the tracks, so to speak, to a one-time car dealership on US 220 about three miles south of town.

Piedmont began in 2005 with Catdaddy, an 80-proof spiced corn-based moonshine. Junior Johnson's Midnight Moon—the result of a partnership between the NASCAR Hall of Famer and Piedmont—evolved a couple of years later. That spirit, which comes in a variety of flavors—peach, apple pie, and raspberry, for example—is available in all fifty states and seven countries, including the United Kingdom, Germany, New Zealand, and China. In the spring of 2016, Carl's Jr. and Hardee's teamed with Piedmont to release the Midnight Moonshine Burger nationwide.

"Our apple pie is the number-one-selling moonshine in the country," says Piedmont founder Joe Michalek, who claims it's nearly bigger than the combination of all the flavors from its closest competitor.

"Our focus is really on quality of ingredients, quality of process, and product taste," says Michalek, a former marketing exec for R. J. Reynolds Tobacco Company. "We're willing to do things that others won't do in order to ensure we have the best-tasting products that can be made."

Junior Johnson's Midnight Moon comes in a variety of flavors—peach, apple pie, and raspberry, for example—and is available in all fifty states and seven other countries.
Photo courtesy of Piedmont Distillers, Inc.

Method + Standard Vodka, which also comes in several flavors, including strawberry and apple spice, is Piedmont's latest release. It's based on ten years' experience making spirits and a focus on ingredients, process, and taste.

To make its vodka, Piedmont uses a proprietary eight-stage filtration process that ends with the spirits passing through a carbon filter made from a coconut shell. Michalek says Piedmont adds a dash of pure cane sugar and infuses the vodka—made from 100 percent corn—with three thousand pounds of fruit for two weeks. "When you taste the base spirit, it's extremely smooth, and then you get a hint of the sweetness that corn brings to the table."

Piedmont is working on a gin—made via direct infusion—which, as of August 2016, had gone through four iterations. The distillery won't release it until sometime in 2017. It's also working on a corn-based aged whiskey set for release in early 2017, which Piedmont will source while it begins to distill and barrel the new spirit.

In the beginning, Michalek says, Piedmont distilled some liquor and sourced grain-neutral spirits, too. He partnered with Johnson, who owns part of the distillery. Not long afterward, Piedmont revved its proverbial engine. At one point, Michalek says, Piedmont was running eight bottling lines, seven days a week. "Now, we're back down to a single crew running every day." The distillery employs more than thirty people, he says.

Buying and transforming grain-neutral spirits made sense for Piedmont in terms of keeping up with demand, as well as producing great-tasting liquor.

"All of our Midnight Moon products use a pure GNS base," Michalek says. "We use a confectionery, baker's-grade sugar, pure cane, no high-fructose corn syrup, and it's a completely different product. We put it through an eight-stage filtration process, and then you literally hand-pack all the fruit into every jar using gourmet fruit, Grade-A quality. No seconds, no parts and pieces.

"Our cost of our product is at least double the other moonshines out there, at a minimum. It is expensive to make it, but that's kind of how we differentiate. When you go and taste our products, you go, 'Wow, it's fantastic.' Other people use the extracts and colors, just squeeze some stuff into the bottle, and that's how they make their stuff, and they make it cheap, and they make it fast.

"You can't make it as pure and as clean as they can," he says, referring to his contract distillers. "We do make some stuff here and process everything here, because it's very different—what comes out of here, than what came in here."

He walks through the distillery. The original German-made still has been, at least for the time being, officially decommissioned. Michalek points to two large tanks, a modern interpretation of a double thumper.

On a shelf in another room sit jar after jar of once-clear spirits, now a multitude of colors, the result of liquor sharing space with fruit. A recipe for gin is neatly typed on a small, square sheet of paper—juniper, orange peel, lemon peel . . .

Toward the rear of the distillery is a pair of ten-thousand-gallon tanks, one of which is used to purify water. Much smaller stainless-steel tanks—seven hundred to eight hundred gallons—line an adjacent wall. The tanks are labeled "Cherry," "Peach," and "Cinnamon." Another says "Holiday Blend," a combination of apple juice and cranberries. All are blended according to weight. Exact and precise.

The bottling line is easily the largest among North Carolina distilleries. A dozen or so workers are filling bottles, Fleetwood Mac's "Go Your Own Way" playing from a speaker.

Piedmont sells a lot of liquor, no doubt. But the distillery isn't driven by profit, Michalek says. He scoffs at talk of the distillery's "overnight success."

"It was very difficult to start back in '05, and it was painful for years," he says. "We almost shuttered it in 2008, right during that whole financial meltdown. We made it through that, and now we're eleven years into this, and you see this explosion of the distilleries, like you saw with the breweries and the wineries.

"I don't think it sustains itself. I know there'll always be a market in North Carolina for North Carolina products. It's hard not to support the home team. But they don't support us everywhere you go across the state either, and we were the very first ones. It's been an interesting dynamic."

He eschews any criticism related to the decision to use GNS. "Our philosophy is, we make it as good as we possibly can, and if we can't make it as good as we could possibly make it, then we'll contract it. We don't have a $5 million or $6 million plant. We've priced it out to do international sales, and it was $5.5 to $6 million to put in all of that equipment, so we've kind of made due with what we've done."

Take, for instance, someone who makes chocolate-chip cookies, Michalek says. "Do you grow your own flour and make your own chocolate, or are you using ingredients? I guess at the end of the day, everyone's got an opinion, and that's what makes the world go round.

"There's a great deal of effort and expense that go into making our products. What's our passion? It's to make highly differentiated, great-tasting products that others won't take the time or the expense to make. You can have an opinion, but at the end of the day we're making world-class spirits, and the consumers are choosing them day in and day out because of the quality and effort we put into it.

"I think it all comes back to the ingredients, to be quite honest with you. I've tasted a lot of the big mass brands that are cheating with either extracts or color additives. The margin and the penny drive the decision making. It's not about exactly how good that product is. They go, 'Sometimes good is good enough.' Then you go to the other side of the spectrum, and you've got all these guys coming into business in their garage operations. They might be growing their own corn and making their spirits from start to finish, and you taste their product and it's not very good. You've got this continuum of small guy, upstart, poorly crafted spirits, and you got the big guys that are just doing everything driven by profitability. You'll find Piedmont is, arguably, slap-dab in the middle.

"Everything is 100 percent natural and 100 percent real. Our focus is on the ingredients, the process, and ultimately the taste, and I would put our spirits up against anybody's in the world."

Greensboro Distilling

115 West Lewis Street
Greensboro, NC 27406
faintinggoatspirits.com
336-273-6221
The distillery offers tours and tastings
from 3 p.m. to 7 p.m. on Friday, from
1 p.m. to 6 p.m. on Saturday, and from
1 p.m. to 5 p.m. on Sunday.

THE LITTLE YORKIE SCAMPERS into Guilford County's first distillery and heads straight for Bill Norman, who reaches down and gently lifts him. The dog is Augustus, though Bill calls him "Augie." He gently pets the dog as he speaks, Augie disappearing in his lap.

It's an interesting juxtaposition—the tiny pet and Bill, in denim bib overalls, bald but with a long beard that reaches to the middle of his chest.

Bill and Augie are surrounded by family. Bill's wife, Shelley, sits on a barstool just over his shoulder. His son, Andrew, is in a facing chair. Bill sips an excellent pale ale from Gibb's Hundred, poured from a sixty-four-ounce growler, which he's sharing with the family's guests. He knows he can pour at will. The brewery is right next door. Augie relaxes, content.

The conversation veers back to the topic at hand. To their distillery and to Fainting Goat Spirits.

Bill mentions a family vacation to Seattle nearly a decade before. During a visit to a local distillery, he turned and looked at his family. They could do this.

"For eighteen years, I was an executive chef," Bill says. "Looking at all of the equipment and everything was just kind of very comfortable to me. About four years ago, we really got serious about it."

The Normans rented their current space in the heart of downtown Greensboro in October 2015 and started distilling their first product, a wheat vodka called Tiny Cat—an endearing term for their children. The vodka is exceptional, buttery with hints of vanilla. Emulsion Gin—a new

Andrew, *left*, and Bill Norman work in the distillery. The Normans rented their current space in Greensboro in October 2015 and started distilling their first product, a wheat vodka they call Tiny Cat, an endearing name for Bill's children.
Photo by Lisa Snedeker

American-style gin, lighter on the juniper and heavier on the cardamom and coriander, with a little German chamomile and some lemongrass, cucumbers, and orange peel—will play off the vodka.

To start.

Andrew Norman, the master distiller, has a passion for aged whiskey—specifically, bourbons, ryes, and single malts, aged in new fifty-three-gallon oak barrels. The single malt—which the distillers are talking about enhancing with fruit woods—will age about a year, the straight rye for two years, and the bourbon for four.

"We're going to do it very traditionally," Bill says. "Most people who make whiskey typically leave it in the barrel for about three months. We know after three months we could probably do something, but we really want to be able to hang on about a year for that single-malt whiskey."

Its barley isn't grown in North Carolina, but Fainting Goat is getting it from a malting company in Asheville. The other grains—corn, soft red wheat, and rye—come from farms in Marshville and Kinston. A shiny new "Got to Be NC Agriculture" sign hangs prominently among the barrels, mash tuns, stills, and fermenters.

"It comes in whole. We mill it down ourselves," Bill says of the grain. "Five days a week, we do a run, and we use six hundred pounds of North Carolina grain every day, five days a week."

He talks about a farmer, accompanied by a boy of ten or so, dropping off grain for the distillery. They were proud of their product, appreciative of the business and the chance for a consistent customer.

"It's easy to grow, relatively, but you've got to know you're going to sell it at the end. To know there's somebody at the end who's going to commit to using it. Makes their life a lot easier as well.

"Because of my background as a chef, I do all of the mash. I do the cooking of the product, and that makes sense to me. With his palate for alcohol, he does all the distilling." He's referring to Andrew, who smiles and shifts in his seat. Everyone laughs.

"It helps with the mash part of it," Bill says, "but chefs are notorious for not following recipes. So, for the distillation part of it, it's a science, and it's got an art to it as well, but that is something better left to people who have the talent for that."

Fainting Goat has a three-hundred-gallon still that includes a four-plate whiskey column, a sixteen-plate vodka column—it had to cut away part of the roof to fit the tall column—a gin basket, and a shotgun condenser. Powered by steam, the still was made by Artisan Still Design of Alabama. The distillery's sixty-gallon still allows for experimentation and innovation. All the equipment is visible from the sidewalk through large windows, on display for people heading to or leaving the restaurants, brewpubs, and coffee shops that define this regentrified wedge of the state's third-largest city.

"You have to have an excitement, you have to have a vibe, you have to have a presence, and a place where people know who you are and what you're doing," Andrew says. "People say, 'You're really making something that's real liquor here. You're not just playing around with stuff.' That is important for us, to be in this environment."

In June 2015, Fainting Goat bought a spot for a thirty-second TV commercial to air during the Super Bowl the following February. "The fact that the Panthers just kept winning, and every game we'd say, 'Oh, my God, they're going to go to the Super Bowl,' was glorious for us," Andrew recalls. "But we knew that even though we were not going to be able to do a call to action and get an immediate response to that, it was important to brand as if we are just already comfortable with who we are as a product, because we are."

A goat walks into a bar. No joke. It's how the black-and-white ad begins. It's a play on the company's name, a respectful nod to myotonic goats, whose muscles stiffen, often causing them to fall.

"When they get excited, they just stiffen up and fall over, with their legs in the air," Bill says. "It kind of describes our family. We're a little bit out there. We kind of scare other people when we do what we do, but we're just kind of comfortable with it and okay with it."

Brothers Vilgalys Spirits

803 Ramseur Street, Unit D
Durham, NC 27701
brothersvilgalys.com
919-452-8924
The distillery offers tours and tastings from
4 P.M. to 7 P.M. Wednesday through
Friday and from 2 P.M. to 5 P.M.
Saturday, starting every hour.

RIM VILGALYS IS BUSY. He has little choice.

Working less than two miles south of Durham Distillery, in a gritty row of small industrial buildings about a block from a set of railroad tracks, Vilgalys's hands are full, figuratively and literally.

Vilgalys studied creative writing at the University of California–Santa Barbara. Now in his early thirties, he looks much younger. His acumen for business, his unrelenting drive, and his inherent charisma are attributes more often found in people somewhat older.

His father, whose family is from Lithuania, is a professor at Duke University, and that's what brought the Vilgalys family to Durham. "I've grown up in Durham and kind of watched the city change a whole lot," Vilgalys says.

A brother with whom he started Brothers Vilgalys has since moved to New Zealand. Although Vilgalys has help—friends, associates, partners—it's immediately clear he doesn't often remain idle. He busies himself running the distillery and all that entails, including writing for his website and making a unique line of Baltic-style spirits he infuses with all manner of herbs and spices, by hand, and which he boils in a two-hundred-gallon stainless-steel kettle, at one time the base for a still.

He begins to speak, then pauses, cognizant of the incessant rattling of a washing machine that sits just inside the tasting room. He apologizes. "Sorry, I have a washer going. I don't know why this place has a washer and dryer."

Rim Vilgalys in his distillery in Durham, where he makes Krupnikas and other liqueurs
Photo by Lisa Snedeker

He acquired the space next door—where he makes his liqueurs—in May 2012. Several months of red tape later, he finally saw his products on ABC store shelves.

"That was the biggest factor getting started, because we didn't know how long the paperwork was going to take," he says. "We had this tunnel to get through before we saw any revenue, and that's the scariest thing, starting this on a limited budget. You might just run out of money while you're trying to tackle the red tape. We got through it in seven months, which is as fast as I've heard of anybody doing."

He refers to the business as "a fake distillery." Like some other stops around the state, Brothers Vilgalys doesn't make its base liquor, a fact he readily shares. Simply bottling ethanol requires a permit to distill, so . . .

"Neutral alcohol is basically a commodity," he says. "Even if we had all the equipment to make it, which we don't, it would still be cheaper to buy it than to make it ourselves.

"I think to a large extent we benefited because our operation was so simple. We weren't trying to make our own alcohol from nothing, and we didn't have these massive plumbing or electrical requirements in the beginning. So we've kind of upgraded our system and the building as we needed to suit what we were doing."

What he's doing—making a signature spiced honey liqueur called Krupnikas—began on a simple stovetop. It's a product with roots in an old cookbook somewhere on the internet—an old Polish and Lithuanian recipe containing wildflower honey and spices such as cinnamon, cloves, nutmeg, caraway, allspice, and star anise. "The drink itself goes back to something like the sixteen hundreds," he says.

"This basically got us invited to a lot of parties. Seeing all the new stuff happen in Durham, it eventually got us thinking, *How hard could it be to set something up like this?*"

Vilgalys walks through a door and into a room with a small desk—his office, a sort of gateway. The main door to the distillery, where visitors enter from a skinny parking lot, is mere feet from the desk. The door, now wide open, presumably swings on time-worn hinges. A set of steps leads outside. A busy roadway is across the lot. A train whistle blows. The washing machine shakes and moans.

Vilgalys traverses the office and enters the distillery. He reaches down and grabs a large bucket, a vessel for the wildflower honey he procures from Henderson, Hillsboro, and Greenville. "We end up buying about ten buckets at a time," he says. "Depending on the size batch we're making, we'll just dump them in this convenient bucket-sized opening." He points to the hole. Five immersion elements heat the kettle, an upgrade from what he calls a "pimped-out" home-brewing kettle, which now sits a few feet away.

"We get it up to a boil, then we will add all the water. Then we add the spices—about a hundred pounds of spice. We'll boil those guys for about six or seven hours, and then we start adding our honey. Once the honey is blended in, we mix it with the alcohol. The Krupnikas will get tucked away in these steel barrels, and we'll let that settle for a few days. We'll rack it to a new barrel before we bottle, and then it goes through the bottling line there."

That process proceeds a few bottles at a time—"basically, all powered by pizza and beer."

The distillery has partnered with Pebble Brook Craft Spirits, which offers its Apple Pie Liqueur and Mystic Bourbon Liqueur, a blend of bourbon and spices. Mystic's distiller, Barrister & Brewer, is building its own distillery in Durham. Vilgalys ages and bottles the products for all three distilleries in the thirteen-hundred-square-foot space alongside the tracks in Durham.

Now, he's back in the tasting room, past the open front door that leads to the office, back to where the tour began, a cinder-block room with a couch and some chairs. It's without pretension. Comfortable.

Vilgalys motions toward four small, colorful bottles at the end of the bar. "These guys," he calls them. Experiments. He'll let the buying public decide. What they like, he'll keep. Otherwise, well, he'll probably try something else.

"They're all a little bit different," he says. "These are lighter alcohol liqueurs, and because we were already set up to do something like our Krupnikas, we just branched out into these other guys."

The other guys: Zaphod, Beebop, Beatnik, and Jabberwock.

"These went through about six months of R and D, where we just kind of brought them to parties and asked people."

Zaphod came first. It includes star fruit, guava, mint, sage, lemongrass, and peppercorns. Try it in a mint julep or mojito, he says.

Beebop—rhubarb, hibiscus, rosemary, allspice, chamomile, coriander—is tart, but in a good way. It's sippable and good with gin. "I kind of copy Campari recipes when we're doing stuff for cocktails. It's not bitter like Campari, but it's spiky, and it kind of stands out in drinks like that."

Beatnik is made with beets and savory herbs—fennel, rosemary, and sage. "Of the new ones that we've come out with, this one has some traditional roots in an old Estonian recipe. That was something we read about, but we never tried any authoritative version of it. So, who knows how close we got to the real thing?

"The process we use for these guys is basically cold maceration, so you get some of the fresher flavors, more of the aromatics, and less of the things you'd get from Krupnikas, which is more suffused.

"We blend everything on the scale, and we're just taking different whole botanicals and stuff to add in there. That's where all the flavor comes, in the case of these guys. The alcohol just works as a solvent to pull those fresh flavors out."

Vilgalys shares the Jabberwock, which comes with a stern warning and a wry smile. "This one's really spicy, so . . ."

Chipotle peppers, manzano peppers, coffee, chicory, eucalyptus, lemongrass. How hot can it be, really? Just take a sip and . . .

"I always try to have my I-told-you-so moment with this one. This one definitely has some heat behind it. It's peppery. It's not that much raw heat, but it does have a lot of peppery spice."

You don't say? It's safe to assume it's one of the hotter alcoholic products on the market, at least in the United States. It's hot in the throat, as peppers tend to be, but the heat builds and lingers. Strong and intense, yet savory—inviting, even.

Memorable, controversial. Again, Vilgalys's words.

More on
Distillers Association

Raleigh Rum Company was little more than an idea when the distillery's owners realized they needed some sage advice. They sought out Top of the Hill's Scott Maitland, whose successful restaurant and distillery are just a short drive up Interstate 40.

Maitland is also president of the Distillers Association of North Carolina.

"He's done nothing but help everyone," says Raleigh Rum's John Benefiel. "When we first started, he brought us in, sat us down, and he was the one that said, 'Look, this is what I've done. This is what you guys need to lobby for with us.' He kind of encouraged us."

Benefiel says Maitland told them, " 'Don't worry about what I have here,' " at TOPO. " 'It may be better to do smaller and just add on when you need more.' He was a good guy."

The association is not unlike the North Carolina Craft Brewers Guild and the North Carolina Winegrowers Association, in that it was formed and exists "to promote the common business and regulatory interests of and to improve the business conditions for the North Carolina craft distilling industry."

The "One-Bottle Law" was a result of lobbying efforts by the distillers' association, which as of late 2016 included thirty-three members. "It has made an incredible difference on so many different levels," Maitland says of the law. "You've got, obviously, the sales that happen in your own place, but the big thing is that now we're getting governmental support. Up to this point, the Department of Tourism wouldn't support it because there was nothing for people to buy once they got here. Now, Tourism is on it, Agriculture is on it. And we've seen increases in sales."

North Carolina distillers pay a modest fee for inclusion in the association.

Charlie Mauney—a cofounder of Southern Artisan Spirits in Kings Mountain with his twin brother, Alex, and father, Jim—expected a growth spurt in the industry, though not so quickly. "Not as fast as it has happened," he says. "When we started, there was nobody, and now it's crazy. Almost every large city has a distillery. The good thing, it kind of grows an entire category as far as craft liquor."

Keith Nordan of Carolina Distillery adds, "The association has gotten a lot more organized. There's actually some funding sitting there for lobbyists, advertisements. The North Carolina Department of Agriculture has been a great plus."

Some members of the association, including Southern Distilling Company of Statesville, had yet to open their distilleries as of late 2016 but nevertheless have reaped the benefits of the collective effort. It goes back to the association's mantra, the idea that rising waters lift all ships.

Vienna and Pete Barger, for example, founded Southern Distilling Company, which plans to open in 2017. Vienna, too, went looking for advice and guidance. In 2013, she called on what was at that time a small band of North Carolina distillers, including Troy Ball, Nordan, Maitland, and the guys at Southern Artisan Spirits.

"They had just formed the North Carolina Distillers Association," Vienna says, "and so I became a part of that organization and really started focusing our efforts, in addition to doing the due diligence and research to establish the business, and working on the lobbying efforts with the general assembly and working on the bottle sales legislation."

The association, thanks in no small part to TOPO's Esteban McMahan, promotes the group through social media and the "NC Spirits" app. The group designated October as North Carolina Spirits Month and promotes tours, tastings, events, and businesses highlighting local spirits.

But there's still work to be done. North Carolina is a control state and will probably stay that way for the foreseeable future. In addition to expanding the "One-Bottle Law," the distillers are pushing for online sales, which will keep tax revenue in North Carolina.

Nurturing a relationship with the state ABC and its boards is key, says Melissa Katrincic, the association's vice president and president and CEO of Durham Distillery. "We're trying to move from us being perceived as a nuisance, because we are booming but we're not help-ing them much yet," she says. "We're trying to work through how to have a great relationship with ABC moving forward and figuring out how we can add to North Carolina spirits wholly."

"It's still slow, it's still young, and I think people are still learning about it," says Fair Game Beverage Co.'s Chris Jude. "When they hear we're a distillery, I get a lot of people that will just be, like, 'I didn't even know that was legal in North Carolina.' It's definitely growing."

Durham Distillery

711 Washington Street
Durham, NC 27701
durhamdistillery.com
919-937-2121
Tours are offered at 4 P.M., 5 P.M., and 6 P.M. on Saturday and some Friday evenings. Call the distillery or visit the website for more information.

LEE KATRINCIC, A PHARMACEUTICAL CHEMIST from Pittsburgh with some twenty years' experience, points toward a desk—more of a work table, really—holding all sorts of interconnected equipment.

"Contraption," he calls it.

It's where he perfects his recipes for gin. Katrincic is the head distiller at Durham Distillery, which he cofounded with his wife, Melissa, the distillery's president and CEO.

Gin was a hobby for the couple. When they traveled, they would seek out new offerings—taste gin, talk about gin, share gin.

Melissa, who grew up in Miami and has two decades of experience in marketing and operations, was facing a layoff. But she had an idea, a plan. She told her husband, and he laughed. Lee found the humor before he realized the potential.

"Let's just make gin," she said.

Her plan made sense, and Lee knew it. They quickly got to work, at least partially aware of the formidable task ahead.

For each batch, the distillery uses about six pounds of juniper berries, an amount impossible to source from Durham County or from North Carolina.

"Gin botanicals really need to be globally sourced," Melissa says. "Even though, with craft gin, you have a lot of artistry you put into it, if you want to be distributed nationally, as well as an export-market potential, you have to have consistency from batch to batch. You don't want our batch 5 to taste different than our batch 10."

Lee Katrincic, a pharmaceutical chemist from Pittsburgh, at the distillery in Durham he owns with his wife, Melissa
Photo courtesy of Durham Distillery

Lee and Melissa learned about distilling. They sought out experts, whom they worked with and alongside. They enrolled in classes in Chicago and Seattle. They bought a small still and began testing recipes. By the summer of 2015, the couple was making gin on Washington Street in Durham.

The Katrincics make 88-proof Conniption American Dry Gin and Conniption Navy Strength, which clocks in at 114 proof. "A big gin drinkers' gin—lots of juniper," Lee says of the Navy Strength. "We balance that with some caraway. There's rosemary, bay leaves. It's pretty savory. Having a 57 percent alcohol product allows us to really load the botanicals in there. If I put this much botanical intensity in something like our American Dry that's 44 percent alcohol, it would be cloudy. The Navy can hold those botanical oils."

Navy-strength gin is typically a product in the United Kingdom, but it's an emerging spirit in the United States. As of May 2016, Durham Distillery was producing the lone navy-strength gin in North Carolina. "It's really fun for distillers, because you have to balance the heat from the alcohol but still have the botanicals," Melissa says.

Durham's Navy Strength Gin recently earned a score of 96 and a Platinum

Medal from the Beverage Tasting Institute, which wrote, "Clear color. Bright, clean, floral fresh grassy aromas and flavors of licorice cream, fig and dried citrus, herb pepper bread, and resinous juniper with an even, vibrant, fruity medium-to-full body and a warming, refreshing, long mixed peppercorns, herbal honey, cinnamon ginger bread, and minerals finish. A lively, spicy gin that will be great in cocktails."

"We really don't know what it means, but it's pretty damned cool," Melissa says.

The American Dry is significantly tamer but no less compelling. "We call it 'a gateway gin,'" Lee says. "If you're not a big gin fan, this is how we help turn you on to gin." The juniper punch, he says, is secondary. A sip brings fresh cucumber and honeysuckle, as well as the required, yet pleasant and fragrant, juniper.

The Katrincics use a different set of botanicals for their Navy Strength

Durham Distillery is near Fullsteam Brewery and Durham Athletic Park, former home of the Durham Bulls and a setting for the iconic baseball movie *Bull Durham*.
Photo courtesy of Durham Distillery

and American Dry Gins, each containing about ten. They use an electric Mueller copper still, manufactured in Germany, to make 90 percent of the gin via vapor infusion. They then employ a unique process for the remaining 10 percent, using a rotary evaporator for vacuum distillation of the more delicate botanicals—cucumber and honeysuckle for the American Dry, figs for the Navy Strength.

It's a marriage, so to speak, of art and science.

In the Mueller still, Melissa says, "we have a vapor tray versus a gin or botanical basket. A vapor tray is fantastic. You have the consistency of heat in the pot, and it's focusing those vapors through the botanicals only. So the gin vapors are what's going through the still, and then come out after they've been reliquified in the condensation column."

The process is efficient, she says. "Our runs take two and a half to three hours, and we get about 250 to 300 bottles of gin."

Lee spent about a year perfecting the recipes. "I individually distilled maybe twenty, twenty-five different botanicals on this contraption here," he says.

Yep, that same contraption.

"I have my pots here with my spirits. This is my basket for the botanicals. I put juniper in there by itself and then distilled that, and had a bottle of juniper distillate. I put coriander in there. I sat there mixing with shot glasses, using eyedroppers to see what tasted good, what didn't taste good. I generated a flavor profile and eventually worked our way up to the still."

Many distilleries, Lee says, get into business to make whiskey, and gin is often an afterthought, a means of making money while waiting for the whiskey to age. "Most distilleries are going to throw some juniper in, throw some stuff in, and hopefully it turns out well."

The Katrincics are in it for the gin.

Melissa remembers her grandfather passing her olives from his martinis. She remembers enjoying the taste, developing a passion for juniper-flavored spirits. "I love gin," she says. "It was always the spirit for our family."

That sentiment played a role when it came to naming the distillery's signature spirits. When Melissa was getting a bit testy as a child, her grandmother would tell her to calm down. "Don't have a conniption," she would say.

The Katrincics now encourage such behavior.

When Durham Distillery got going in the summer of 2015, the Katrincics often turned to Rim Vilgalys with questions—about the ABC, about doing business in Durham, things like that. They've become good neighbors and are making it work in a city undergoing a positive transformation, although things on Washington Street are a bit quieter than over at Brothers Vilgalys Spirits. A bit more gentrified.

Fullsteam Brewery is around the corner and just this side of Durham Athletic Park, former home of the Durham Bulls and a setting for the iconic baseball movie *Bull Durham*. The Pit—"Whole hog, pit cooked over charcoal and wood," its website boasts—offers North Carolina barbecue in the most genuine of forms. Roasted pork, pulled or chopped. It goes great with beer and a cordial for dessert. Chocolate, maybe? Coffee with a twist?

In all, Durham Distillery makes three liqueurs—all labeled "Damn Fine," all made from grain-neutral spirits, and all around 32 proof.

The mocha, which Melissa says, is "amazing with bourbon," is made with dark chocolate from Videri Chocolate Factory and cold-brewed coffee from Slingshot Coffee Co., both in Raleigh. Nothing artificial, and as locally sourced as possible.

Melissa talks about how some chocolate liqueurs—some of the world's biggest sellers—use artificial flavors and colors. "We use only natural ingredients," she says. "We melt about twenty-six pounds of chocolate at a time. Which takes only, oh, five hours or so but smells amazing. We hand-temper it, and we make simple syrups. They all have their own different sweeteners"— turbinado sugar in the chocolate liqueur and orange blossom honey in the coffee liqueur, for example—"but there's nothing artificial in any of them."

Try it on ice cream, she suggests. Or in a martini.

"Even bars are realizing now they can do just half our chocolate and half vodka and do a martini straight."

No syrup needed.

Top of the Hill Distillery

505-C West Franklin Street
Chapel Hill, NC 27514
topodistillery.com
919-699-8703
Tours of the distillery are offered most
 Thursdays at 6 P.M. and 7:30 P.M., as well
 as most Saturdays, though times vary.
 Visit the website to book a tour.

Top of the Hill Restaurant and Brewery is a landmark at East Franklin and North Columbia Streets in Chapel Hill, on the edge of the University of North Carolina campus. One of the state's first microbreweries, TOPO is also noted for its organic craft spirits, produced a few blocks west in a building once occupied by the *Chapel Hill News*.

Esteban McMahan is the "spirit guide" at Top of the Hill Distillery. The operation was started by Scott Maitland, who is McMahan's business partner and the proprietor of TOPO Distillery.

Maitland and McMahan, both army combat veterans, set up a state-of-the-art German distillation system made by CARL Artisan Distilling and Brewing Systems of Stuttgart, which has been making stills since 1869. Engineers and distillers in Germany can jump online and adjust TOPO's continuous-column still, which strips the alcohol from the mash in about six and a half hours, versus about four days in a traditional pot still, which would also suck ten or twelve times more energy.

McMahan, a former fund manager with solid roots in the Triangle area, had saved some money and decided to "take a few years and see if I can make a go of it and have some fun," he says. He pauses and smiles. "I figured I've been drinking professionally about twenty-five years. It would be fun to try to learn a little bit about it and to do this."

McMahan and Maitland offer a contrast in styles. McMahan has long, dark, flowing hair; Maitland keeps his light hair cropped short. Both men have strong builds, though McMahan resembles a slot receiver and Maitland more of a linebacker. But their commitment to seeing this distillery succeed is in march-step.

The German distillation system made by CARL Artisan Distilling and Brewing Systems of Stuttgart, in TOPO Distillery in Chapel Hill
Photo courtesy of Top of the Hill Distillery

The distillery produces the hyper-aged Eight Oak Carolina Whiskey, the clear Carolina Whiskey, an organic vodka, and the 92-proof Piedmont Gin, which includes juniper, coriander, rosemary, cinnamon, red lemon peel, star anise, and cucumber.

All of TOPO's spirits are made with organic soft red winter wheat, which, says McMahan, makes for a much smoother alcohol compared to corn, for example. That sweet, smooth wheat comes from Jack H. Winslow Farms, less than a hundred miles east of Chapel Hill in Scotland Neck.

A "Reserve" two-year barrel-aged whiskey was, as of May 2016, still on the way. That whiskey, McMahan says, could well be the world's only locally sourced, organic, 100 percent wheat-mash-billed "straight" wheat whiskey. "It's pretty rare to find locally sourced whiskeys. It's even rarer to find organic locally sourced whiskeys. And it's that much rarer to find organic locally sourced whiskeys aged for two years in barrels. It's really fantastic. The wheat is a much better base for alcohol than corn. We're really excited about getting that out."

TOPO's distilled products became available in 2012 and are attracting wide attention. In addition to North Carolina, they're available, for example, in Pennsylvania, Alabama, and Utah. The distillery produced twenty-three hundred cases of liquor in 2015 and expected to produce nearly four thousand in 2016. On weekends, it hosts tours that draw as many as 150 people.

"They're all world-class spirits," McMahan says. "It shouldn't matter that they're distilled in North Carolina. Our goal is to be a world-class distillery that's located in North Carolina, using North Carolina agricultural products."

TOPO's vodka, in fact, earned a five-star rating—the highest possible—from F. Paul Pacult's *Spirits Journal*. "Clear as rainwater," Pacult wrote, according to the TOPO website. "I favorably respond to the toasty, grainy smell of wheat snack crackers that greets you after the pour. . . . It is rare that I come across an unflavored grain-based vodka with as much layering, depth of flavor, character and ribbony texture. Tasty enough to quaff neat and slightly chilled."

TOPO makes a line of spirits including vodka, whiskey, and gin.
Photo courtesy of Top of the Hill Distillery

"Very few vodkas get five stars from him," McMahan says, "and we're very proud of that."

TOPO whiskey is distilled to 80 percent ABV, the vodka to 95 percent. Both spirits are chill-filtered. TOPO also charcoal-filters the vodka and gin but not the whiskey, as "it would remove the character that we want," McMahan wrote in an email.

The tasting area and the distillation room are separated by a wall of glass, the state-of-the-art equipment from CARL Artisan Distilling taking as much space as an old Goss Community Press, if this were still a place where people produced newspapers.

Now, it's where 4,000 pounds of wheat turn into about 5,500 liters of mash, which turns into about 600 liters of vodka, 650 liters of gin, or 700 liters of whiskey. It's where TOPO mills and grinds the wheat, where distillers cook it. Where they add hot water and enzymes, and where the starches become sugars. Where it's cooled in a chiller, and where it goes into a fermenter with the yeast. Where, after about five days, it becomes an alcoholic wash, somewhere around 11 percent. Where the wash is heated again, at which point it looks, says McMahan, "like a big pot of cream of wheat, bubbling like crazy."

The spent grain goes to a farmer in Orange County for compost and feed for hogs and poultry. TOPO uses a former dairy machine to fill its hand-labeled bottles five at a time, one cork at a time.

Organic, local, sustainable.

McMahan reaches toward a barrel of the upcoming "Reserve," about two years old as of May 1, 2016. He stops to smell "the angels' share"—the whiskey evaporating from the cask, which amounts to a small percentage each year. He knows the wheat whiskey will be good. Smooth and complex.

McMahan encourages visitors to taste TOPO's spirits alongside high-profile national brands. He challenges them to compare and contrast. TOPO's Carolina Whiskey is the base for the 92-proof Eight Oak, a reference to the combination of oaks and toasts used in the hyper-aging process, which happens in a stainless-steel tank.

"So many people like their whiskey because it burns," he says. "Well, whiskey shouldn't burn. It should have great flavor. You should feel the heat, but it shouldn't burn in your mouth like rubbing alcohol. You want the flavor, and you want the taste. You don't necessarily want burn."

Fair Game Beverage Co.

193 Lorax Lane
Pittsboro, NC 27312
fairgamebeverage.com
919-245-5434
The tasting-room hours are 4 P.M. to 8 P.M. on Friday, 1 P.M. to 7 P.M. on Saturday, and 1 P.M. to 5 P.M. on Sunday. Tours are given 6 P.M. on Friday, 1:30 P.M. and 3 P.M. on Saturday, and 2 P.M. on Sunday. Call or email the distillery to reserve a spot.

CHRIS JUDE AND KEVIN BOBAL HAVE SET UP SHOP at a British-themed restaurant in Greensboro, where visitors have gathered around a long table near the bar to sample a new offering from Fair Game Beverage Co. in Pittsboro. They aren't there to taste fortified wine, rum, or brandy. They're here for a mysterious little pepper—the *aji dulce*, or Tobago.

Sure, people love Fair Game's spirits, but the distillery had a problem. Those spirits take time to make, time spent mostly aging in bourbon barrels. Six months, twelve months, fifteen months.

"We were talking about the challenges of that," says Bobal, the distillery's sales and development "ringleader." "A, you have a lot of money, inventory sitting on the rack. B, we can't bottle it too soon. It has to age."

The state ABC sold out of the apple brandy, and it took several months for the distillery to restock the shelves. Not a bad thing to happen, but . . .

Six years ago, Jude, Fair Game's head distiller, learned about the Tobago pepper from a farmer whose property lies adjacent to the distillery. Jude took the unique and rare fruit to his liquid lab.

"He brought some samples in for us," Bobal says, "and we were all just blown away by it."

Jude infuses the pepper into Top of the Hill Distillery's soft red organic wheat vodka. Fair Game calls it "The Flying Pepper." "It's a real clean vodka," Jude says, "and that's important because you want to get the pepper right out

Ringleader Kevin Bobal, *left*, and master distiller Chris Jude at Fair Game Beverage Co. in Pittsboro
Photo by Lisa Snedeker

front. The flavor really comes through, and it's something fun to highlight."

The Tobago, although related to the wickedly hot habañero, is instead sweet and smoky. Bobal likens the taste of the raw pepper—supplied to Fair Game by several North Carolina farms—to a stick of Juicy Fruit gum.

"There's really no other vodka out there on the market quite like this," he says. "When you see a pepper vodka on the shelf, typically it's something that's going after a spice or a big black pepper flavor. No one's capturing this type of flavor profile.

"What's really cool, I'll take them home to cook with, to put on salads. I just pop them into my mouth and eat them because they're that flavorful. That little *aji dulce* pepper is so flavorful, and nobody has used it in a spirit. There's no alcohol bite on the front side. You smell it, it smells like a habañero. You think the heat is coming."

It doesn't come. It just isn't there. It's more cotton candy and fresh-baked cookies and bubble gum.

"To me, sorghum and the *aji dulce*, or Tobago pepper, are two of my favorite foods," Jude says. "It just works so well in the vodka."

Certainly, someone else will catch on. Someone with lots of money for marketing and advertising. Someone who can produce not just barrels but tanker trucks of the stuff.

So be it.

"We're trying to do a real good job of being the guys in first position with this," Bobal says. "They can call it a Tobago vodka, but it will never be the same thing because the way we branded this was really around the name, The Flying Pepper. You don't even know it's Fair Game until you look at the bottom of the label, where we take a real backseat to the branding because we wanted The Flying Pepper to be its own entity. It will never be The Flying Pepper. That's ours."

At the bucolic distillery in Pittsboro, Jude is always in motion. Moving, searching, experimenting, finding. Bobal would probably prefer that Jude hone in a wee bit more on the existing products.

"I do like change. I do like new things, and I like creating stuff," Jude admits. "I'm learning that we need to . . ."

Bobal, who is standing nearby, finishes Jude's sentence: "Focus."

They laugh. It's obviously an inside joke.

Fair Game is just southwest of the Triangle. The state's major interstate highways surround the distillery on all sides. But figuratively, at least, they're hundreds of miles away.

"It's all agriculture around us," Bobal says. "No hustle and bustle of streets. Crows, hawks, tractors—that's typically all you hear out at our place."

"We do a lot of work directly with farms," says Jude. "I would say 80 percent of our raw materials are coming from North Carolina farmers."

"We're using as much North Carolina agriculture as we can," Bobal says. "We're embracing North Carolina farmers as much as we can in developing all of our products."

Fair Game makes fortified wines—such as Scuppernong Tipper and port-style Ferris Red—using grapes from the Haw River Valley. It also produces Apple Brandy, the aged Amber Rum, and a rum called No'Lasses, made from sorghum that Jude grows and distills in an alembic copper-pot still. The distillery's latest release is the limited-edition Carolina Agricole Rum, a style native to the French Caribbean, made with pressed sugarcane juice and aged in used bourbon barrels.

"We do spirits and we do wines," Bobal says. "We're using all North Carolina agriculture in all the things we're producing. The fun part of my job is, everybody loves all of our products. Our products are a little bit unique, but everybody loves the flavor of everything we're producing."

Now, on a spring Saturday, Jude takes a few moments to host a tour. To do this, he leaves the tasting room, where he and another bartender for hours have poured beers, wine, homemade sangria, brandy, and rum. The beer taps, which dispense several local products, consistently run dry, sending Bobal out on a glorified beer run to retrieve yet another sixtel.

Jude says the Pittsboro distillery is often busy, although this Saturday is different. It's the grand opening for the Pittsboro Farm and Forest Trail, a mile-long swath weaving around the distillery and adjacent farms. An organic farm on the property is serving dinner this evening, and people have crowded into the tasting room beforehand. Jude helps to fill orders and direct guests.

In the distillery, it's much quieter, calmer. Jude is in his element. He points to a large closet just to the left of the front door. "My research cabinet," says Jude, who studied sustainable agriculture and renewable energy technology at Appalachian State University and who for a time worked at a biofuels company on the distillery property.

The building that houses the distillery is one of several in a compound at the end of Lorax Lane, surrounded by farms, an orchard of pears and apples, wildlife, and woods miles from town. Oddly, the distillery building was at one time used in the production of military alloys. The company departed years ago, but it left behind this structure, which includes a foot-thick blast door, explosion-proof lighting, and explosion-proof vent fans. A blast would, by design, explode outward and leave the roof and ceiling.

Jude points to barrels racked in several rows along a wall. It's where the Amber Rum ages, in charred oak barrels that once held Kentucky bourbon.

The rum shares traits with Fair Game's No'Lasses. About 15 percent of the sorghum Jude uses is grown at a friend's farm in Silk Hope, about thirteen miles northwest of Pittsboro. The two began raising sorghum, which can grow as tall as fourteen feet, several years ago. Jude says some of the distillery's sorghum comes from Denton, North Carolina, but most of it is from a large farm in Tennessee. Few farms in the United States grow sorghum in bulk, he says. Most North Carolina farmers relegate sorghum to an acre or so.

"It's kind of a cult thing," he says. "It's an old heirloom sweetener, and a lot of chefs are into it. You can find it in the country, all across the Southeast."

Jude makes the rum with organic panela sugar, a raw sugar from Colom-

Fair Game pays homage to the harvest, which dovetails with a season of fairs, fun, and parties.
Photo by Lisa Snedeker

bia made from evaporated juice from the cane.

"I'm pretty excited about the recipe with this," he says. "I like a funky rum—a lot of flavor, grassiness, wildness. I wanted a nice raw sugar, and this panela, you get a totally different flavor out of that, as opposed to blackstrap molasses."

Jude makes the No'Lasses, though not technically a rum, using rum yeast. "You press the cane, you get the juice out, and you cook that down to molasses. Sorghum molasses doesn't have any sugars removed, whereas blackstrap cane molasses, they process it and remove sugar crystals. So it's kind of a little sweeter but with a similar vegetal flavor. It's got a little bit of whiskey character, too. You get a little bit of peat or grassiness out of it.

"My goal with all of these is to make brandy that you can sip, a rum that you can sip."

The Amber Rum currently available aged for fifteen months, though future batches probably won't age as long. "We just didn't have the production or aging timeline balanced out," Jude says. "It's a really nice rum. I'm really happy with it—a lot of big flavor. Kind of floral, a little briny, kind of a *rhum agricole*. I kind of like that wildness to it. Rum just kind of fascinates me, the No'Lasses and this. I love getting all the flavor out of it."

The rum, No'Lasses, The Flying Pepper, and the Apple Brandy all run around 80 proof, or 40 percent ABV.

Jude races to keep up with the spirits' soaring popularity. He's used to it. The Apple Brandy, in fact, sold out of the ABC inventory at one point. Like Fair Game's other spirits, the brandy is distilled in an alembic copper still and aged. The distillery, in responding to the shortage of its Apple Brandy, tripled production. Jude says, "It's apple brandy with apple wine aged in a bourbon oak barrel, so you kind of get this bourbony-apple character out of it."

The distillery's port-style Ferris Red includes Cabernet Sauvignon, Merlot, Chambourcin, and Norton, as well as imported Toriga grapes for sweetness. The brandy and the Ferris Red are aged in bourbon barrels for six to twelve months, the Two Step White—made with Chardonnay and Seyval Blanc grapes with a touch of Palomino, a traditional grape for sherry—up to a year and a half.

The Apple Brandy is smooth and has a crisp, lasting bite. The distillery's Scuppernong Tipper is infused with brandy. Like Fair Game's other fortified wines, it pays homage to North Carolina's native grape. Serious wine drinkers often eschew scuppernongs because of their cloyingly sweet character. Not this one, as much of the candy-like traits have been expelled.

"We started with limitations in this business," Jude says. "We were really set up to be juice-based, brandy-based. The rum fits in nicely. We weren't able to handle grains, so it forces us toward these more unique styles of spirits, away from a bourbon whiskey or a moonshine or something like that. And I like that, but I do want to make a malt whiskey. I'm talking to some local brewers about making a malt beer and then distilling that." Heavy on the rye.

Bobal doesn't hear Jude talking about the whiskey. His attention is focused on a group of purple martins that are flying in and out of a cluster of synthetic gourds attached to a high pole overlooking the distillery and a row of greenhouses.

"They're migratory birds, here for a few months," says Bobal.

Jude takes a quick glance before making his way again to the tasting bar, across a narrow gravel road now filled with people headed for dinner. Always moving. Rarely standing still.

Raleigh Rum Company

1100 Corporation Parkway, Suite 132
Raleigh, NC 27610
raleighrumcompany.com
919-307-7725
Free tours and tastings are offered at
2 P.M. every Saturday.

It's a Saturday in June, and temperatures that were once barely comfortable are racing higher, toward a feverish North Carolina summer.

Just east of the busy Interstate 440 Beltline in Raleigh is a run-of-the-mill industrial park. Offices and warehouses, those types of things. Mostly standard and nondescript.

Mostly.

One business stands out. A wide-open door welcomes small bands of people, who step in and out of the space, which is about the size of a commercial garage. They relax on couches and chairs that are arranged on the concrete floor to facilitate conversation, to promote a feeling of community, if only for a few hours each week.

That was the plan.

Friends John Benefiel, Matt Grossman, and Chris Mendler grew up in the area and all went to college in the Triangle. They often met at the Flying Saucer, a venerable beer bar in downtown Raleigh, where they laughed, dreamed, and disagreed. Somebody mentioned starting a brewery.

That market was packed already, they felt.

But spirits?

"Can we open a distillery here in Raleigh?" says Benefiel, recalling the conversation. "What would we call it? Raleigh Rum Company?"

Sure, that worked.

"It was a two-minute conversation. We said, 'This is a great idea. We can do it.' Our wives hated it, but we did it anyway."

Rum mash fermenting at Raleigh Rum Company
Photo by Lisa Snedeker

The friends moved into their current space in July 2014 with the help of a Kickstarter campaign. They set things up and waited. By 2015, Raleigh Rum was in business with one relatively small electric six-plate copper reflux still.

The initial pallet of 82-proof White Rum left the distillery in May 2015. It lasted in ABC stores for about two weeks, which introduced an interesting problem. A pallet took about three and a half weeks to produce. The partners' second pallet, says Benefiel, sold out in a week, the third in three days. The fourth . . .

"We didn't even make it into the inventory because it was already sold."

So the friends bought a second still, which was pretty much identical to the first. Sounds easy enough. But the progression from idea to bottled rum stalled after the friends tasted it.

"Our first fermentation batch was absolutely terrible," Benefiel says. "The next five were absolutely terrible. And then we kind of ironed it out. We tried all different types of combinations."

Recipes were tossed, reimagined, and reworked. Eight or nine times. The distillers decided to soak the white liquor in oak chips as a means of mellowing and flavoring the spirits.

"It was good, but it wasn't smooth enough," Benefiel says. "It wasn't that it was bad, but there was just something that was missing. We really wanted to smooth it out. You could still taste the alcohol—the heavy alcohol. When we put it on the oak, it really just pulls out a lot of those flavors, really mellows it out. Then we distill it again. It really flavors it, really smooths it out. It's delicious. The problem now is that it's a brown-white rum. You can't have that. So we run it through the still again."

Distilled. Aged. Distilled.

"That kind of sets us apart from others."

Raleigh Rum settled on a pairing of sinisterly dark blackstrap molasses and brown sugar. Bright and silky with a lingering sweetness. It has hints of tequila, Benefiel says. "That's because of the sugars. It's not over-refined. It's a very simple, very easy recipe, but more of a traditional, pirate-style, if you will, drink."

Barrels filled with rum age at Raleigh Rum Company, which shipped its first pallets of white rum in May 2015.
Photo by Lisa Snedeker

The distillery released its Spiced Rum, using the White Rum as a base, in December 2015. The Spiced Rum includes ginger, vanilla, cinnamon, cloves, and cayenne and is aged in barrels donated by Fullsteam Brewery in Durham.

"We leave the cinnamon in there right about a day, a day and a half, and then we let everything else steep in there at least three days," Benefiel says.

The distillery is aging some of its White Rum for at least two years and is working on a dark rum that will place more emphasis on molasses.

The rum—all of it—ferments in forty-five-gallon plastic totes in a separate room adorned with local paintings, located just off the distillery. From behind a small bar in the distillery, Benefiel offers tastes to friends, rum lovers, tourists, and people who may have just wandered by.

Small, local, friendly. He's determined to keep it that way, although the friends—also busy with families and other jobs—have hired a sales and marketing specialist, Michelle Koch, who took one of their tours and convinced the men she could bring a fresh perspective, as well as specific expertise and experience.

"If we need more, we just buy another small still and keep growing," Benefiel says. "Even if we quadruple in size, we really won't be a tenth of the size of a major distiller.

"We're going to go the small route. We like the taste, we like the flavor profiles of the smaller stills, and this is how we're going to continue to roll."

Pinetop Distillery

1053 East Whitaker Mill Road
Raleigh, NC 27604
pinetopdistillery.com
Check the website for information about
  tours and tastings.

It started with a New Year's resolution between friends: create a bottle of liquor before year's end.

Innocent and fun, but why stop there?

Jon Keener was in on that resolution. He started talking about it, and other friends got interested. A business, if you will, began to ferment.

"Why go at it half-ass? Go at it full bore, and do something real with it," Keener says. "Being from North Carolina, we wanted to be as locally sourced and North Carolina–centric as we can, and really try to create something unique that harks back to the way things used to be made, when it was really handcrafted."

The result is Pinetop, a slang term for moonshine and an ode to the state tree of North Carolina, the tall and majestic longleaf pine.

Keener calls Pinetop "a raw whiskey," a classic bourbon recipe made with grains from Chatham and Wake Counties. "The labeling and bottling is set up to reinforce and evoke that. We're North Carolina proud. We've got everything we need here to produce great spirits.

"We're grain-to-glass guys," he says. "We're not buying industrial-produced alcohol and just kinda flavoring it. North Carolina has a very long liquor tradition, legal and illegal. We're trying to take it back and do it the old way, pre-Prohibition."

Before wood distilling became long on shortcuts. Before the proliferation of liquors distilled primarily with sugar.

Pinetop plans a gin using its base whiskey, which is made using a 70 percent corn blend, as well as 15 percent barley, 10 percent wheat, and 5 percent

The distillers describe Pinetop as "a raw whiskey," made from a classic bourbon recipe with grain from Chatham and Wake Counties.
Photo courtesy of Pinetop Distillery

rye. "Just so there's a little bit of a bite in it, and you know you're drinking whiskey," Keener says. "We were adamant about not dumping sugar into it, to short-circuit or jump-start the ferment process. By using all naturally produced sugars from those grains, once I ferment it and proof it off, you really get the flavors of those grains. When it's a majority sugar recipe, or when it's just a corn and sugar recipe, the only flavors you get are that real burn.

"That *white lightning* name came from the burn of the sugar. When you take the sugar out of the recipe, you instead taste the softness of those grains. Instead of having really hot, burny moonshine, or having a really corny liquor, you end up having something with a real depth of flavor. Even unaged, you can really enjoy and taste the differences. We tried to make something unique so that people will enjoy drinking it."

Pinetop has a custom-built continuous still that can run twenty-four hours a day, as opposed to traditional batch distillation. The liquor is distilled a second time with a fractionating column, which works much like a reflux still but with some subtle differences.

"The reason I like that is, one, it's not $250,000 in startup costs," Keener says. "And two, because I'm not batching it, I'm continually running it, and I get a much smoother product coming out. Call it using classic, traditional recipes produced with modern equipment in a modern way to produce a really consistent and smooth-flavored liquor. That's really what we're going for."

Eventually, the distillers will release an aged product—or, as Keener calls it, "a proper whiskey."

All of the partners are from the Raleigh area. The distillery is in an industrial-type space housing several businesses just inside the northeastern corner of the I-440 Beltline. Lynnwood Brewing Concern is a next-door neighbor.

The partners have spent their first several months in operation making and distilling mash. Tours and tastings will come.

"You just got to crank and get it done," Keener says, referring to ABC requirements. "But prettying it up so my wife would actually go in there, that's what we're working on right now."

Seventy Eight °C Spirits

2660 Discovery Drive, Suite 136
Raleigh, NC 27616
78cspirits.com
919-615-0839
Visit the website to schedule a tour.

Donald McIntyre buys lemons by the case. Then he zests them in a nondescript shop in Raleigh, part of a strip mall of stores that are mirror images of his own, many of them empty. Others, like McIntyre's, are devoid of signs. He's a tough guy to find.

He points out a mistake in the Craft Distillery Trail passport—his and a distillery with a similar-sounding name are transposed on a map in the booklet. Somebody with a passport noticed that. He shrugs.

McIntyre calls his business Seventy Eight °C Spirits, a reference to the boiling point of pure ethanol. McIntyre zests the lemons—at one point in the spring of 2015 he bought seventeen cases, 165 lemons per case—to make Limoncello, his initial offering. He followed that with a Limoncello infused with jalapeño extract and his Blood Orangecello. All come in at about 58 proof. Although the alcohol content is relatively low, all are unique and equally interesting. The citrus is prevalent in each. The jalapeño is present, yet the heat plays only in the background, leaving the fruit foremost on the palate.

"We were watching one of these food shows a couple years ago, I guess," McIntyre says. "My daughter couldn't watch most prime-time stuff, so she likes to watch food shows. We were watching this food truck thing, and these guys had jalapeño lemonade. I said, 'Hmm, that sounds good. Let's make some.' So we made it, and it was really good. And I said, 'Hey, I should put jalapeño in the Limoncello.'"

Donald McIntyre
discusses blending
his Limoncello at his
distillery, Seventy Eight
°C Spirits.
Photo by Lisa Snedeker

It's his bestseller.

"That's kinda the cool flavor, jalapeño," says McIntyre, who is forth-coming, yet interestingly reserved. His hair has grayed, matching his beard. People who taste the blood orange liqueur like it the best, he says, but ABC stores have been slow to pick it up.

He's been in business since 2014. So far, sales have been fair, he says. "I didn't think it would be this hard. It's hard to get in anywhere. It's hard to get people to change what they normally drink."

True enough. But McIntyre's offerings are worth a sip, if for nothing more than a pleasant change in direction. Author Henry James said the words *summer afternoon* were the two most beautiful in the English language. Sip a Limoncello and remember that sentiment.

McIntyre isn't a salesman, a title to which he doesn't lay claim or hope to hold. He's a chemist—organic and later pharmaceutical. From Syracuse, New York, he's been in North Carolina since he was twelve. He worked for a large company, which merged with another company. He banded with a group of coworkers to form another company. But business got tough. "I ended up going back and forth over whether I should do this or not. My wife finally said, 'Either do it or get a job,' so I spent lots of money to do this."

He stands in the production room, one of a few in an otherwise austere shop. On a table before him are a dozen or so clear-glass decanters—in the shapes of footballs, menorahs; there are others, but the aforementioned stand out—which he can't use because they won't hold the proper volume of liquor. It's frustrating, he says.

But then he begins talking about making his Limoncello. His mood brightens.

He talks about macerating his product in stainless-steel drums, using a base of lemon oil—in the case of the Limoncello—and ethanol. He talks about how the zest is in nylon bags, about how he adds water and sugar and uses motion to speed maceration, which doesn't take nearly as long as his early research suggested. He talks about how he uses jalapeño extract to keep the flavor consistent, and about the lengthy government process, since the extract required approval. He talks about how he lost an entire batch waiting for that approval.

He talks about making an orange liqueur, about how he took to a neighbor a liqueur he made with Valencia oranges and a store-bought liqueur highlighting blood oranges. The neighbor preferred the blood orange.

He talks about lemons, about how he has to store his supply in a distributor's cooler until he can get to them. "We have to zest lots of lemons, and we do it all by hand. Initially, we had this instrument, it was kinda like an apple peeler. It would take the zest off the lemons. It did a pretty good job. I ended up wearing out the blades, we did so many lemons. I could never find the blades again. Come to find out, the company has gone out of business. So then we had to switch over to the potato-peeler-type deal. It's similar to that. It has a serrated edge, so it will just take the zest and not the pith."

Five cases at a time. That's about McIntyre's limit. "You do five cases and you're, like, 'That's enough.'"

His bottling system is near the door. It's a pump system. But because his liquor is more viscous than, say, a vodka, he would probably prefer something else.

"It's a little problematic, pumping it. I think gravity-fed would be a lot better."

The Farmer-Distiller Relationship

The idea of growing, raising, and consuming crops, fish, and live-stock with a focus on sustainability isn't exactly, well, fresh. Yet words such as *local* and phrases such as *farm-to-table* are ubiquitous. Today, knowing the farmers who grow your corn or raise cattle for your favorite restaurant is cool. Hip and trendy.

The advent of farming goes back about eleven thousand years, to the Middle East's Fertile Crescent, according to research by population geneticists at Harvard Medical School, published in the journal *Nature*. So we've been doing it awhile. North Carolina has some 48,800 farm operations, encompassing about 8.3 million acres, the 2015 state agricultural overview says.

"The local food movement has caught up with what people have been doing for years," says Paul Jones of the North Carolina Department of Agriculture and Consumer Services.

Though North Carolina corn production fell in 2015, from 103 million bushels in 2014 to about 82.5 million—a drop of about 20 percent, attributable in part to lower commodity prices and less acreage—the state's farmers still harvested 730,000 acres of corn, according to the U.S. Department of Agriculture. Meanwhile, an increase in acreage allowed sweet potato farmers to increase production by 3 percent. Farming is oftentimes a matter of family and tradition. Farmers, through good times and bad, proceed with a passion and dedication driven by a culture of optimism and the hope that things will be better next year.

Signs promoting "Got to be NC Agriculture" adorn the walls of distilleries around the state.

"It's our objective to make sure that working farmlands continue to exist, and I think distilleries and wineries fit nicely into that objective," Jones says. "Distilleries and wineries use agricultural products grown in North Carolina by local farmers. They offer value to crops that may not be right for fresh markets. Plus, many of the distilleries and wineries are located on farms or near farms."

For reasons primarily economic, yet inherently altruistic, a good number of North Carolina distilleries rely solely on products grown within the state. They also typically return spent grains and excess fruit to local farmers to feed livestock.

Recycle and reuse.

"We do grain fermentation," says Andrew Porter of Doc Porter's Craft Spirits in Charlotte. "We ferment on the grain, we distill on the grain. So, afterwards, we pump our stillage into those square totes, and every week a different local farmer comes and picks it up. We do the same thing that breweries do. The farmer feeds it to his calves, pigs. He gets about six hundred gallons of our spent mash every week. We just give it to him for free. We're really trying to stay green, trying to recycle everything."

The farmer-distiller relationship is mutually beneficial, a partnership bound by trust and a shared vision of success.

On a busy fall football weekend in Chapel Hill, Top of the Hill Restaurant and Brewery can serve as many as fifteen hundred to seventeen hundred diners a night, says Esteban McMahan. A desire to go local can come with pitfalls. A decade or so ago, says McMahan, TOPO owner Scott Maitland and one of the area's largest producers of free-range chickens talked about supplying chickens to TOPO—about a thousand breasts each week. The rancher could offer just a small fraction of that. "That supply chain wasn't in place back then," McMahan says. "Now, it is, but back then it didn't exist.

"We were struggling with that. We wanted to keep the money in North Carolina, not ship it all out-of-state. That's one of our frustrations with beer. With all the talk about beer in North Carolina being local, 99 percent is not local in the foodie sense. All your basic ingredients—the hops and the barley—are coming from a long way away. We were frustrated by the fact we'd be shipping all of that base-ingredient money out-of-state again."

The TOPO team wondered what else it could do. It considered wine, but that would take too long. Spirits? Now, that might just work.

Jack H. Winslow Farms in Scotland Neck was at the time an anomaly among farmers, McMahan says. A large-scale grower of organic wheat, the farm was struggling, its organic wheat acreage down to about seventy-five acres. "It was about three and a half times more ex-

pensive" than non-organic wheat, McMahan says, "and he wasn't finding enough people to buy it."

But once TOPO and the farmer took the next logical step, the result was an uncommonly smooth, clean Carolina whiskey.

"All you need is world-class grains or fruits, which we have plenty
of in North Carolina," McMahan says. "All we need is world-class distillation equipment, and we should be able to make world-class spirits. It
doesn't matter where you're located."

Lassiter Distilling Company

317–319 North First Avenue
Knightdale, NC 27545
lassiterdistilling.com
919-295-0111
Tours and tastings are offered from 11 A.M.
to 5 P.M. on Saturday. More information
is available on the distillery's website
and Facebook page.

Gentry Lassiter of Lassiter Distilling Company in Knightdale doesn't have a background in science. Or engineering, for that matter. "My background is in marketing and communications for a pharmaceutical company.

"We've got kind of an interesting story," he says. "Unlike a lot of folks who are in distilling, we don't have a family history in it."

Gentry, an equal partner in the business with his wife, Rebecca, has for a long while enjoyed well-crafted spirits. He began to visit distilleries to learn how great spirits are made.

"But I hadn't thought to make it myself until I went on some tours and really found that the people who are doing this, even though it's a really hard business, are really enjoying themselves. Aside from the fact that making liquor is pretty cool, it's a fun business to be in, too. It's something that our family is involved with, and we really like that."

The Lassiters are focusing on rum. Their first release, Lassiter's North Carolina Rum, is an unaged spirit made entirely at the distillery, from molasses sourced from Louisiana sugarcane. They employ a custom-built hybrid stainless-steel electric still, set near the front of an austere room down a hallway from the tasting bar. The "rum" column on the still, Gentry says, includes ten perforated plates.

"Rum, I think, is where you're going to see the most activity, especially at the craft level, in the next five years or so," Gentry says. "Vodka is a mature market, in my opinion. Whiskey is a saturated market, but it seems to keep growing. And gin is kind of experiencing a renaissance right now.

"Rum is still in its early stages. You're starting to see more folks come in to making rum. A lot of that, I think, is because it doesn't require the same kind of equipment to make grain-based spirits. So you'll have a lot of those kind of actors. But I think you're also going to have a lot of people who really look at rum as a very versatile spirit."

Gentry was born in the Triangle but moved away when he was young. He returned in early 2016 and from all indications is here to stay. The distillery quickly got its federal license and obtained its North Carolina license that August. By the fall of 2016, the Lassiters' rum was stocked in the Raleigh warehouse. The Lassiters bottled batch number five as Hurricane Matthew began moving across the state and into Raleigh. The distillery was unscathed.

"I learned how to distill by studying," Gentry says. "We did not do any

Lassiter Distilling Company is open for tours.
Photo courtesy of Lassiter Distilling Company

The first release from Lassiter Distilling Company is North Carolina Rum, an unaged spirit made entirely at the distillery from molasses sourced from Louisiana sugarcane.
Photo courtesy of Lassiter Distilling Company

illegal distilling prior to getting into this business, so it was a real leap of faith on our part, and on the part of my investors.

"We really just decided that this is something we want to do, that we feel like we have a good time doing. And so far, that's proven true. We're quick studies, and we enjoy marketing products, and I think that's what you have to be ready to do if you're going to make it in this business."

Gentry calls his rum versatile and complex. It's sweet but not overly so. "We do all of ours in one single run, so it has a really unique character to it, a lot of nice floral and citrus notes. You can really taste the molasses in it, but it's also a very clean rum that does well in any cocktail. That's really what our rum is designed to do—to stand up in some of the world's greatest cocktails.

"Frankly, I'm sure that anybody who makes liquor will tell you that theirs is the best. But I honestly believe that our rum is the best that you can buy right now. It's absolutely delicious, and I really enjoy making it. And that says a lot for someone who has spent a lot of time tasting and making his own rum. I figured I'd get sick of it after a while, but so far I haven't."

The Lassiters will begin aging their rum at some point. They're thinking about liqueurs and flavored rums. But the kinds of flavors they choose will depend on a number of factors, including—and maybe primarily—the taste of the collective market.

But that's the future. For now, Gentry's hands are, in his words, "kind of full."

Broadslab Distillery

4834 NC 50 South
Benson, NC 27504
broadslabdistillery.com
919-207-1366
Tours are offered at noon, 2 P.M., and 4 P.M.
on Thursday, Friday, and Saturday. Visit
the website for more information.

JEREMY NORRIS IS WEARING A GRAY T-SHIRT adorned, in black block letters, with a couple of words: *Broadslab Distillery.* His elbows rest on the wooden surface of his tasting bar, the smooth and polished veneer reflecting the glass-encased lights hanging from the ceiling.

Norris leans in and starts to talk. The words are sincere, reverent.

"I was raised right here, and we used to run a produce farm right here. We used to grow produce all out here in these fields, and we had a produce stand under that oak beside the road. We sold everything we produced right there under that tree."

Corn, squash, cucumbers, tomatoes, snap peas, field peas, snow peas, onions, Irish potatoes, broccoli, beets, turnips, collards.

"We had it all."

We.

Norris and his grandfather Leonard Wood. Wood raised Norris. He taught him about hard work, about farming, and about life. He showed him how to make whiskey.

In Broadslab.

The story of the community goes, according to Norris, like this: Broadslab in the 1700s was a road that ran through the farm between where NC 50 and NC 242 lie today. Carolina bays—marshy elliptical depressions in the ground—saturated the area.

"When it was wet, the wagon wheels would mar up, the horses would mar up. It was a mess. It was a hellhole, basically. So what they did, they took the broad slab off the pine trees at the sawmill. That first outer cut that's

rounded, with the bark on it, they'd take the flat side and turn it up."

Heart pine, he says, takes forever to rot, so they laid it down and made a slab road all the way through the area and started calling the community Broadslab. It was a place of free-spirited, rebellious, hard-headed people.

"If they got crossed up, there were no lines," Norris says.

Wood often told Norris stories about his great-great-grandfather, how he would make whiskey and take it on his wagon to Fayetteville, to be shipped via the Cape Fear River.

"This was before Prohibition, in the 1880s," Norris says. "My granddaddy had told me about all that stuff. And we're in Johnston County. That says enough. Not to mention Broadslab. This is the hotbed of Johnston County for bootlegging."

Sheriff C. L. Denning estimated that, during the sixty months he had been in office, he and his deputies destroyed six hundred whiskey stills with a total capacity of forty-five thousand gallons, according to the *News & Observer* of Raleigh in a recent report taken from a story originally published in 1950. "Johnston County's top law enforcement officer believes enough whiskey and beer were found on raids during that period to fill a farm pond," the story said.

"My granddaddy always told me, when I was coming up . . ." Norris's words trail off, evaporate. He's thinking about his grandfather.

"In Broadslab, everybody in this neighborhood back in the thirties, forties, fifties, everybody was bootlegging. Percy Flowers was the biggest bootlegger in the county, as far as any one bootlegger, but there's probably more liquor made in this end of the county, because everybody did it."

Again, he stops.

"Moonshine Capital of the World," he says.

He may be right. But so may the Calls in Wilkes County. Or the old 'shiners in Franklin County, Virginia.

Doesn't matter, really.

"It's not as big as it was," Norris says of making moonshine. "But it's still vibrant."

He has a photograph taken in 1951 or 1952 of the early Mule Days, an annual festival in Benson. It shows a group of men—all "characters," Norris says. All Broadslab boys, who, toting guns, planned to place a still on a trailer and run a batch as they slowly drove the parade route. A whiskey float, of sorts.

Their plan didn't come to pass.

"When you mentioned Broadslab, you automatically thought bootlegging, because everybody that lived in Broadslab either made whiskey, drank whiskey, or sold whiskey. It was a rough place."

But as Norris grew up, Wood—long since tired of running from the revenuers—turned his focus on his grandson, on the farm. He started work on the building that presently serves as the distillery's tasting room and retail store, now filled with the work of local craftsmen, as well as hats, T-shirts, and the like. His plans included a produce outlet and a place to live, toward the rear of the building. The porch had once been a greenhouse, large rolling doors providing the gateway from inside.

"He would sit in the greenhouse and pot plants for the garden, and be in his living room at the same time."

But Wood never finished the project. He got older. Norris's grandmother became ill. And Interstate 40 led potential customers away.

"Before 40 was built, 50"—the state highway—"was the route to the beach, so we had all the beach traffic. In the eighties, we had a really good business. Then, in 1990, they opened up Interstate 40, and it dried up the business. I think that's the reason why he built this, to kind of take it up a notch and be more of a draw. But it didn't work."

When Norris was in his early teens, Wood, considering the county's—and the family's—history, suggested his grandson think about developing a moonshine museum on the property. "He said, 'I bet you people would come off the interstate out here to look at it.'"

Norris shrugs and laughs. "I was thirteen."

In the 1800s, the farm sat on a four-hundred-acre parcel. As the generations passed, Norris says, the land was split up and sold off. "It was down to thirty acres left in the family. In 2005, I got the chance to buy sixty acres of it back."

The farm continued to grow. Norris planted row crops. He farmed them and sold them.

"I lost money one year, broke even the next year, and figured out real quick there's no farming small. You've got to have a niche, a value-added commodity. So I started thinking, *What am I going to do to justify keeping this land without selling it or developing it, to make it profitable, make it sustainable?*"

About that time, North Carolina got its first distillery.

Norris began to learn about the industry. He studied brands, processes.

"I learned then about neutral-grain spirits. I didn't know anything about neutral-grain spirits. So I got to figuring out then how the business worked, how they rolled. You kind of got different classes of distilleries.

"I thought to myself, *If I build a distillery out here on the farm, out here where my great-great-granddaddy's house was . . .* This thing started growing in my mind, and I said, 'I'm going to do this. If I build this distillery on the farm, I'll be able to sell every drop I can make because it's so unique and unusual.'

"That's where I was wrong. I figured that out years later."

He laughs again. Shakes his head. He's doing quite well now, even if the phrase "doing well" is purely relative.

He built a distillery in a structure two thousand feet from the highway and just about as far from the tasting room.

"There was an old farm path that went in there to it. Muddy, beat up—a little, narrow path. So I built a road, a nice, big, wide road that tractor-trailers could get in and out of. Myself. When I say I built it, I actually built it. That road probably took me a year, messin' on it to get it right.

"Then I built the building. We drew the still up, designed the still, me and my granddaddy. I got a local welding shop down here to help me build the still, and I put in all my infrastructure and everything. I tell people it took me four years to put all the infrastructure in place to get a license, physically and financially. I finally got licensed in November of 2011. We filed our formulations, labels, got in the marketplace August 1, 2012."

Two weeks later, his grandfather checked into a hospital. He died a couple of weeks later, on September 1.

Norris recalls his grandfather's story. He talks of how Wood remembered all of the small details. Places, people, dates. He wishes he could remember more, that he had written things down. He wishes he had bought a recorder and used it as Wood, seated on a pickup tailgate, cajoled and encouraged Norris. Taught him. Raised him.

"You don't even consider them dying. Hell, it didn't cross my mind."

Much of what Wood told him remains with Norris in a corner of his mind, like an old box of dog-eared baseball cards stashed in an attic. Memories mostly hidden but there when he needs them, when he wants to remember.

"Like my granddaddy always said, 'Son, you got the water you need. You got the perfect water. It will make the best liquor.'"

That water—pure and perfect—is from a fifty-foot well dug by hand and marked by a small wooden building just feet from the distillery.

"I had the name, I had the history, I had the farm, I had the recipe. I got the water. I had everything. I had the know-how. I grew up around it. Everything comes natural. I didn't have to go to school. It was a fit."

Getting a product on the shelves was a large part of phase one.

Broadslab makes its Legacy Shine using malted non-GMO corn, malted barley, cane sugar, and yeast.
Photo by NCDA&CS

"I thought the cash flow was just going to come in," Norris says.

The second phase included more work on the distillery, a tasting room, and a gift shop.

"Phase two never came. It didn't take off like I thought. I underestimated. I had a good product, a good package, a good story. I had everything. But I had no money or time for marketing. I was busy farming. I do all the distilling and everything myself.

"So I actually did pretty good for two years, if you want to call it that, being no more prepared than we were for marketing, just because we got a lot of good publicity. We kind of hung around for a couple of years in the marketplace, struggling, basically hanging on. I got to thinking, *I need to open up to the public, so people will find out about this place.*"

Norris started to "patch up" the building for tourists. Some window-panes had fallen out. The roof had holes. Some wood was rotten. He found termite damage.

"I got into it, and it was a lot bigger project than just patching up. So I spent a lot more money on it than I thought.

"We opened up, and within a few months the crowds had gotten bigger. We built a tram to take people to the distillery. The brand grew last year right smart, by just word of mouth, organic growth. So now we're in the process of turning this into a restaurant and bar.

"That's my whole goal, my whole thing. It wasn't about money. It wasn't about building to sell it. It was about keeping the farm sustainable, offering the people a true, authentic product and experience. Building this thing up so I can give it to my boys, and they have a reason not to sell it and keep the farm."

Broadslab makes its Legacy Shine using malted non-GMO corn, malted barley, cane sugar, and yeast. Its 90-proof Legacy Reserve moonshine is aged with re-charred American white oak from Johnston County. Its 50-proof Appleshine is infused with pure apple juice and organic cinnamon. In a move toward diversification, Norris makes an unaged "silver" rum that he calls Carolina Coast, as well as an 80-proof spiced version.

"I grow all my corn," he says. "I started growing my barley now. I'm kinda limited to what I can do because all my stuff is 100 percent natural. I don't use any artificial colors, flavors, sweeteners. I don't do any of that stuff. I soak that corn for about two days and let it swell up. I do about a thousand pounds at a time. It's probably more work fermenting the corn than it is distilling it."

Again, Norris's thoughts turn to his granddaddy. He remembers Wood saying, "'I used to make two different kinds of liquor: one to sell and one to drink. That one to drink is a lot of damned trouble. It takes a lot of trouble to make it, but it's worth it. If you'll do that, you'll stick out.'

"I said okay," Norris recalls.

Norris fires his still much like his grandfather did, employing a firebox in a method akin to wood-curing tobacco. "You get this firebox going, and the heat has to go under the still—an old-timey pot still—up the backside, around both sides, all the way around it, and to the exhaust. There's a lot of opportunity to exchange that heat. You don't have to worry about scorching because there's no direct flame on it. It's a neat concept."

The alcohol vapor becomes liquid by way of a "shotgun" condenser composed of 250 tubes, each about three-eighths of inch in width, running vertically, all cooled with well water—"as cold as it can be," says Norris—which drains into a pond on the farm. He gets about a gallon of high-test alcohol every couple of minutes. From a still that began with some drawings on a piece of notebook paper.

"There's some so-called moonshines being produced in these column stills," Norris says. "It tastes like vodka. It's too neutral. You don't get any corn. You don't get any flavor. You don't get that moonshine taste. In this area, there's never been a bootlegger that I'm aware of that had other than a pot-type still. To be moonshine, it would almost have to be in a pot still. It is a different product."

In his youth, as Norris tells it, wild scuppernong grapes grew in woods across the road. At twelve or thirteen, he picked them. He and his friends would make wine, which they'd pour into jugs and sell to migrant workers.

"That was my first experience with producing any alcohol. From there, you catch the bug."

On the way from the tasting room to the distillery, driving on the road he built, Norris slows his pickup. He stops. He points to a still—the sort of display one might find in Williamsburg, Virginia, or at Disney World.

His grandfather recognized the site because of the cork oaks, the only spot on the farm in which they grew. This grove of cork trees is his grandfather's last moonshine site.

"When I built this road, it come right by it."

Happenstance.

Norris steps on the accelerator, drives a bit farther, and parks a few hundred yards away, at the distillery. He's still talking about his granddaddy.

Covington
Spirits

301 Kingold Boulevard
Snow Hill, NC 28580
covingtonvodka.com
252-747-9267
Call the distillery for information about
tours.

It's lunchtime on a steamy Friday in June, and Jimbo Eason is deep into a heaping plate of fried trout. He's in a booth at Beaman's restaurant off Highway 58 South in Snow Hill, the county seat of Greene County, in the coastal plain east of Goldsboro and north of Kinston. The restaurant reflects the town. Unpretentious and genuine. Rustic and friendly.

Eason sets aside a small Styrofoam container, which a short while ago held cooked cabbage. He's holding court, chatting casually about two of his favorite things: vodka and sweet potatoes.

Eason founded Target Marketing and Importing, a broker for wines and spirits. He represents Covington Gourmet Vodka, distilled from—you've probably guessed it—*Ipomoea batatas*, or North Carolina sweet potatoes.

"'The Best Yam Vodka on Earth.' It's gluten-free and Putin-free," Eason says.

Catchy and funny.

But yams and sweet potatoes aren't the same, right?

"A true yam," according to the website of the North Carolina Sweet Potato Commission, "is a starchy edible root of the *Dioscorea* genus," typically brought from the Caribbean. But most people see sweet potatoes and yams as one and the same. And most canned "yams" are indeed canned sweet potatoes. It's almost a case of semantics, but the federal government pointed out the discrepancy as Covington tried to win approval for its label. Eason helped to set things straight.

North Carolina is the top producer of sweet potatoes in the United

States. More than 40 percent of the national supply comes from the Old North State, according to the state agriculture department. Sweet potatoes are gluten-free and loaded with nutrients, including Vitamins A and C, as well as fiber, complex carbohydrates, and antioxidants.

"Sweet potatoes have been used for distillation for centuries in Asia," Eason says. The best *shochu*, from Japan, and *soju*, from Korea, are made with sweet potatoes, he says.

"It's a carbohydrate, but it's our carbohydrate, our starch. It's what we grow around here.

"Most of the vodkas in this country come from corn. Why is that? Because we grow a lot of corn. It's a corn country. You go to Europe, most vodkas are made from wheat, predominantly wheat. If you went to Ireland, Russia, or Poland, more potatoes and sugar beets. You do with what you got, to turn it into alcohol, whatever the category may be. We decided sweet potato, and it's working."

Eason, a vodka aficionado, worked for Skyy Vodka as it began to get a foothold in the marketplace, before Campari purchased the label.

Covington is a popular variety of sweet potato. To make vodka, the sweet potatoes are picked, puréed, and distilled. The process starts with Yamco, which produces aseptic purées from, for example, pumpkins and carrots, as well as sweet potatoes, which because of their soft skins are picked by hand.

"When you go to the store, all you see is a one-shape sweet potato," explains Paul Gussenhofen, production manager at Yamco. "You never see the big, long things, the fat things, oblongs. All the other ones? What do they do with them? If they can't sell them to a hog farmer, they've got to grind them back into the field as fertilizer. So now they just wasted the labor of pulling them out, the labor of sorting them, and now the labor of putting them back in the ground.

"Purée can care less what it looks like. Any shape or size, it doesn't make a difference. So, instead of putting them back in the ground and wasting all that money, they ship it to us, and we make it into purée."

Yamco was started by a group of longtime farmers. Two of them—Jimmy Burch and Bobby Ham—also own pieces of Covington. Yamco uses a patented microwave process to make the purées, which it sells to companies that produce things such as baby food, sweets, and beer, including Sam Adams.

"If you're familiar with moonshining at all, they do their mash, then they have to strain it—they don't show you the straining process—and

The distillery uses twenty pounds of sweet potatoes in every bottle of Covington Gourmet Vodka.
Photo courtesy of Covington Gourmet Vodka

then they go ahead and put it into the kettle," Gussenhofen says.

Using purée eliminates the need to strain the mash, which includes sweet potatoes, enzymes, and water. The process eliminates most waste.

"If you're familiar with canning industries, or heating and pasteurization, the amount of time it takes to heat the product, pasteurize it, cool it down, bag it, you're looking at six to eight hours. I heat mine up in less than ten seconds, and I cool it down just over that," Gussenhofen says.

"By doing it that fast and that proficient, the color, flavor, and nutrition are optimal. The more heat you use and the longer you apply it to it, the more color, flavor, and nutrition you lose. The whole industry's roughly 43 percent of the natural product," meaning over half the values are wasted. "I'm 98."

Yamco seals the product, which in ambient storage has a shelf life of three years. Sometimes, seals break or what comes off the line must be discarded and used for fertilizer.

Someone had a thought. Instead of losing that money, why not make alcohol?

The distillery uses some twenty pounds of sweet potatoes in every bottle. The recipe was developed with the help of the artisan distilling program at Michigan State University, which analyzed purée for things such as sugar content and recommended enzymes for fermentation. "We stayed up there for a week and made our first batch of product because we didn't have a distillery at that moment," Eason says.

The distillery quickly came together. Covington produced its first batch on Thanksgiving Day 2012. Its first case came off the line in January 2013.

Covington uses a multiple-plate vodka column made by Vendome to extract the ethanol, yet retain the flavor of the sweet potatoes. The distillers take care to ensure their vodka has a unique character.

"We get a lot of sweet potato essence transferring over into our product," says Eason, "whereas in other carbohydrates like corn or wheat, there's basically nothing there to transfer over. It's pretty neutral by itself."

Covington uses every part of the sweet potato except the peel. "We want to keep as much of the sweet potato flavor in the finished product as possible, so we don't filter the hell out of it."

"They say that vodka has no color or flavor," Gussenhofen says. "They're right on the color. It's clear. The flavor? Anybody who drinks anything knows every vodka has a flavor, some distinct flavor. This one gives it a little caramel to a butterscotch."

Covington is aging its sweet potato vodka in new oak barrels, experimenting with different chars, and testing at different stages. The distillery has barreled some three thousand cases of sweet potato liquor.

Technically, it's not whiskey because it isn't made with grain. "Distilled spirit specialty," Eason says.

The distillery, which is separated from the purée plant by a series of doors, is incredibly warm. The purée plant is hotter still. On the line, a machine is chopping pumpkins, separating seeds. Workers remove the stems—which can act like loose rocks in machinery, says Gussenhofen—with precision and alacrity.

Few tourists visit the plant. A meeting room also serves as the tasting bar—more accurately, the tasting table—for those who do visit, though a bona fide tasting room is part of the plan.

"We're not getting a lot of traffic out this way. We thought that Walmart Express out here was really going to bring people into the town, but it hasn't really done that."

Eason laughs, takes a sip of tea, and finishes off his casserole, made with wholesome, locally grown sweet potatoes.

Mother Earth Spirits

311 North Herritage Street
Kinston, NC 28501
motherearthspirits.com
252-208-2437
Mother Earth Brewing and Mother Earth
   Spirits offer free tours Tuesday through
   Friday on the hour from 10 A.M. to 5 P.M.
   Saturday tours are on the hour from
   1 P.M. to 8 P.M.

KEVIN GRAHAM HAS STOPPED WORKING, if only for a few minutes. These moments are typically elusive, and he's taking full advantage.

He leans into the bar, hoists a glass of craft beer fresh from the Mother Earth tap. He looks around the polished space, which Stephen Hill patterned after one of his favorite spots in London. The crystal blue façade of the bar, set off by a row of lights dangling just a few feet above, is a pleasant contrast to the exposed brick walls. It's ornate, yet simple. Comfortable. Cool.

It's also a reflection of downtown Kinston, a town of about twenty-one thousand with a history rich in tobacco, textiles, and minor-league baseball. The history will remain, although the tobacco and textiles have faded. The baseball team, an affiliate of the Cleveland Indians, left in 2011, but the town was set to get a new team in 2017.

Kinston is re-emerging on the strong shoulders of people such as chef Vivian Howard and brewery founders Hill and Trent Mooring, who are building a sturdy base for sustained growth. It has become a city of art and culture. A city of food, beer, and whiskey.

"It's really coming around," says Graham—or, to those who know him, "Big Shooter." "That last seven, eight years, since probably Chef & the Farmer"—Howard's noted restaurant—"started up. Since then, not just Stephen investing in the area, other people are investing. It's becoming a place people want to come. It's really good to see."

PBS star Howard and her husband opened Chef & the Farmer in 2006.

Distiller Kevin "Big Shooter"
Graham at Mother Earth Spirits
in Kinston
Photo by NCDA&CS

Mother Earth, which offers some of the finest handcrafted beers in the state, arrived in 2008.

Together, the brewery and distillery occupy a handful of buildings downtown, many dating to the 1880s and all at one time or another scheduled for demolition. The brewery, in fact, was the first local structure to be awarded LEED (Leadership in Energy and Environmental Design) Gold certification from the U.S. Green Building Council, according to a 2013 news release. "That focus led to the installation of solar panels, recyclable carpet, eco-friendly tile," the release says. "The brewery also recycles everything from spent grain (feed for cattle) and the bags the grain comes in (converted to stylish shopping bags by local artisans) to the old wooden bourbon barrels the brewery uses for aging (converted to building materials and art pieces displayed throughout the facility)."

The brewery is situated in a 1950s-era drive-through pharmacy. Millennials dominate the brewpub, swallowing Weeping Willow Wit by the pint and agonizing over First World problems.

"My neighbor, matter of fact, grew up here," Shooter says. "She said you'd drive in and stop your car" at the pharmacy. "They would come to your car, get your list, and they'd get your stuff for you and bring it back to your car."

The solar panels heat the water for the distillery. Plants in the rooftop garden drink their fill of rainwater. Old blue jeans provide insulation, and toilets flush with water from a cistern. The walls, roof, and part of the bar are made from pallets and staves. "We recycle, repurpose, or reuse everything."

Mash for whiskey is born in the brewery. "It's a short process because we don't have to boil it," Shooter says. "It goes straight from the mill to the mash tun, does a mash rest, and we cool it to eighty and take the fermenter to the distillery. It has to be separate. Once it starts becoming alcohol, it has to be in a separate bonded space."

The distillery is compact even for North Carolina—about the size of a well-appointed residential kitchen. "This is my hole, right here," says Shooter, who relocated to North Carolina from California wine country.

Mother Earth bought the forty-five-gallon still from a brewery that planned to use it but never did. "We got lucky, got a really good deal on it, although it was too small. From the get-go, it was too small. Seven days a week, I'm running. I'm going to put a cot back here."

The distillery—well, Big Shooter, mostly—makes gin, rum, and whiskey. He, like some other North Carolina distillers, starts with grain-neutral spirits for the gin, but "the whiskey is all from scratch," aged in fifteen- and twenty-three-gallon barrels.

"We started distilling about three years ago and started putting the whiskey away," Shooter says. "Distilling's still really young, and it's that avenue where you can actually do a craft. You can make something exceptional."

Something such as the distillery's American contemporary gin, which he makes by macerating the fruit, herbs, and spices in the alcohol in large stainless-steel barrels before distilling. "It's light on juniper, but it finishes with citrus," Shooter says. The gin contains star anise, Szechuan peppercorns, cardamom, and orange and lemon peel, among others things.

"I'll drink it on the rocks, and you'll have one flavor. Then you can add soda to it, then all those middle earth tones—the angelica root, the orris root, and those kind of things—come out. And then you can put a tonic with it, and you've got all that citrus in there. It's really, really good."

Shooter is quiet now. Thinking, pondering. He raises an index finger, heads toward another room at the distillery, returns with a pair of unlabeled bottles filled with brown liquid. One is fig and raisin whiskey, a riff on the beer of the same composition, a Belgian dubbel that's part of the brewery's special Window Pane Series. It's a fall beer aged in whiskey barrels.

"So we had some left over, about thirty gallons. I ran it through the still, and then I put it on wood. It's made mostly of wheat, barley, and very little hop. It has almost a brandy smell to it, and the finish and taste. Next year, we're going to do a big batch. I'll barrel it, and the following year, for the release, we'll put out a specialty whiskey.

"I'd like to do more specialty whiskeys, some specialty gins. This is something we were playing with."

The other bottle? A hop liqueur, made from a brewing staple, the beautifully bitter and citrusy centerpiece of voguish IPAs. Hops were cultivated by the British—so one story goes, anyway—to inhibit spoilage on long journeys to the Indian colonies. Now, lush beds of hops grow in a garden located off an alley to the side of the distillery. The garden supplies the owners' restaurant, Ginger 108, which serves sushi made from a sustainable supply of fish.

"We're going to change some things in this," Shooter says of the hoppy spirit. "We're also going to use local honey instead of just regular sugar, eventually."

Mother Earth will expand because it has to. Safety regulations and fire codes might eventually compel it to leave downtown Kinston. Or it might depart for no other reason than to meet the ravenous collective thirst.

"I work seven days a week in here because we can't keep up. We're already looking at expansion, but it's going to take some time. Demand has made us buy bigger fermenters. We were using those little ones down there. There was just no way."

The small copper still and column aren't going anywhere, though.

"This will always stay here. This will always be in production. This little still makes gin like crazy. You can run gin here all day long. It just makes tons of it."

Part of the reason for Shooter's frenetic schedule is Brian Roberts, a mixologist who worked at Chef & the Farmer.

"He's a fantastic mixologist," Shooter says. "He came to work for us, and now he's out in the field. Sales have skyrocketed because he gets out and does what we're doing here."

Roberts promotes the whiskey, gin, and rum. That's what Shooter means.

"He lets people taste it, fall in love with it, and now it's crazy. We can't keep up."

Walton's Distillery

261 Ben Williams Road
Jacksonville, NC 28540
waltonsdistillery.com
910-347-7770
Call the distillery to schedule a tour and
   tasting.

Donald Walton Jr. was raised in Jacksonville. It's home. His family's roots are buried deep in the coastal soil. He went to college at the University of North Carolina at Wilmington, about an hour south on US 17.

Walton decided he wanted to be a lawyer, but then something came up. A relative asked if he wanted to live in Kentucky, to help with the family retail business.

So he went to Kentucky.

He stayed there, seduced by a culture dominated by thoroughbreds and—especially for Walton—bourbon, which runs through every seam and chasm in the Bluegrass State.

Bourbon, according to the website of the Kentucky Distillers' Association, "is a $3 billion signature industry in Kentucky, generating 15,400 jobs with an annual payroll of $707 million." Bars and restaurants in the state feature pages of bourbon offerings. Bourbon-themed events and festivals pepper community calendars.

Walton earned that law degree, from the University of Kentucky in Lexington. The school shares the city with Town Branch Distillery. Four Roses, Woodford Reserve, and Wild Turkey are a short drive west.

"All the time I'm living out there, I'm going around visiting these distilleries," Walton says. "There's a whole bunch of them right there within probably a sixty-mile radius. I had my favorites that I would go to more often than not."

The university, Walton says, keeps records on scores of distilleries, including those that succumbed during Prohibition. He pored over the files. "I got the bug," he says.

But his relative sold the family business, and Walton was left to work for the new owner.

In the late 1980s, he returned home to North Carolina to practice law and to look into starting a distillery, which at that time would have been the Tar Heel State's first since Prohibition. The process was bewildering. The state procedures were haphazard, and the lack of encouragement left Walton disheartened.

Not that he gave up. He set up a corporation in 2005 and, in his words, "started putting the pieces together."

Walton wanted to make bourbon but found that prohibitive for myriad reasons. The emerging bourbon craze left barrels in short supply, which translated to higher prices. Then there was the whole aging thing.

"I looked to a whiskey, and I had made a couple friends that worked for the larger distillers. They suggested I consider a toasted oak chip versus a barrel. I could do a flash aging and have a product for sale."

Walton tries to simulate the process of distilling bourbon, though he reduces the time it takes to age in oak from a couple or more years to two months. "I've tried it four months, I've tried it six months, I've tried it one month. And two months, to me, is the sweet spot."

He distills E. M. Walton's Corn Whiskey—named for his great-grandfather and made with corn grown in Onslow County—five times, ages it on the chips, cuts it to 80 proof, and filters it three times. "We worked on this thing about nine months," Walton says.

He offered it to his friends, and they enjoyed it, partly because it was free but mostly because it was good.

"I'd number the jars where I wouldn't even know what they were. The majority of them went with the corn, and I thought, *Well, hell, the corn is the easiest for me, so I'll just go corn.*"

Walton doesn't cook his corn. Rather, he combines scalding water and seventy pounds of corn grain in blue totes, which are agitated to remove the starches. "I think the cookers are more efficient, but this is definitely the cost-effective way. I can make an unbelievable amount of mash in a short time, just heating this water up and scalding that grain."

The stainless-steel electric still has a 325-gallon tank, which typically carries about 275 gallons for a run, producing 30 to 35 gallons in five hours. The fifth distillation is done by way of the moonshine still. "When it runs

Donald Walton Jr. sells a variety of spirits, including Junior Walton's Authentic Carolina Moonshine, from his distillery in Jacksonville.
Photo by Lisa Snedeker

through that copper, I think it sweetens the alcohol. It definitely changes the taste."

Sometime during Walton's whiskey adventure—the aged whiskey hit ABC stores in the spring of 2015—a cousin stopped by to visit. Walton's distillery sits off Highway 53 about ten miles due west of downtown Jacksonville.

Norwood Rochelle sized up the distillery. He had some thoughts, which he expressed to Walton. "Let me show you how to make moonshine," he told Walton. Rochelle told his cousin he has been making it for fifty years. In the woods. Using cane sugar, wheat, rye, and corn.

Now, a small, 150-gallon natural-gas-powered copper pot still is tucked neatly in a separate corner of the distillery, across the way from Walton's stainless-steel column. It's a bit more utilitarian than the column. Unrefined and unpolished.

"It's real moonshine," Walton says. "If you bought moonshine in this area back in the day, it would probably be the same thing. From area to area, you'll have different recipes, but that's what most of the 'shiners around here use. He told me what he needed, and I set up that little copper still."

Although Rochelle has passed away, his recipe and methods remain as flawless as his 100-proof moonshine, which Walton named Junior Walton's Authentic Carolina Moonshine, after his grandfather, whose hand-sketched likeness almost dares drinkers to try to sip slowly. They can turn that likeness away from them, but then they have to deal with Rochelle, whose picture is on the back.

"We have not thrown away one cup of moonshine," Walton says of the runs since Rochelle took charge. "It was tried and true. He could do it blind-folded, I believe."

It's a hot day in Jacksonville, the heat invisible, oppressive. The stifling humidity is even worse in the distillery, where workers take frequent breaks.

It's cool in the tasting room, the tin walls and dim lighting providing a rustic, yet comfortable, backdrop for sipping whiskey and moonshine.

A first iteration of the tasting space included baseboards and clean trim. "It just didn't look right," Walton says.

Hard-fiddling bluegrass plays in the background, much like it does at the Calls' distillery in Wilkesboro.

Tradition.

Walton hosts bands in the distillery. Bluegrass bands. "I don't play anything here but bluegrass."

A couple drinks hesitantly from a glass at the tasting bar. All the while, a constant stream of water from a model still gently competes with the music, the conversation.

"Apple pie," the couple says almost in unison.

Kitty Walton's Apple Pie Moonshine was named for Walton's great-grandmother, E. M.'s wife. It's an inviting and easy-drinking 30-proof concoction made with cinnamon and nutmeg.

The couple, tucked up close to the small bar, says something about sipping the sweet liquor after dinner, about how it goes down like iced tea.

"Apple Pie gets everybody," Walton says.

Diablo Distilleries

245 Jim Parker Road
Jacksonville, NC 28546
diablodistilleries.com
910-545-7010
Call the distillery or visit the website to
schedule a tour.

PHILLIP O'HARA MAKES WHISKEY THE OLD-FASHIONED WAY, in a still he built with the help of a friend.

His whiskey is a reflection of that copper still. Clean and effervescent. Genuine and traditional. So much so that O'Hara's distillery defies maps, GPS, and point-by-point directions.

Diablo Distilleries, northeast of Jacksonville, is tough to find. The pavement ends and farm fields begin. One loose-gravel road leads to two more, which run toward more open land. A wrong turn leads to an even more unstable gravel road en route to a rocky summit, where all roads end.

O'Hara is waiting at the distillery, a converted farmhouse.

A fine place to make whiskey.

The 234-gallon still is the centerpiece. It's nine feet tall—including the witch's hat—and three and a half feet around. O'Hara talks about making the still, about pounding copper until his forearms ached. He brings up the still's head, which, if made in a certain style, can impart notes of pepper and fruit.

"You'll notice in my clear whiskey, hopefully, you'll taste a little dried Granny Smith apple, a little dried peach," says O'Hara, whose distillery is less than ten miles north of Camp Lejeune.

O'Hara makes corn whiskey using yellow corn from a farm in neighboring Carteret County, which he grinds at the distillery.

"Originally, a few years ago, I started out and had a sour mash, and I had about 5 percent rye in there," he says. "I made up some brown whiskey then,

Phillip O'Hara, also an avid home brewer, founded Diablo Distilleries near Jacksonville. *Photo by Lisa Snedeker*

and I realized two years later that little bit of rye helps the flavor."

He added the rye back in and released the new 80-proof Charon's Oak Whiskey, hyper-aged with oak chips, in the summer of 2016. Charon, in Greek mythology, ferried the dead over the Rivers Styx and Acheron.

O'Hara changed the label and bottle, which had looked like a moonshine jug and featured the word *Shine* instead of *Whiskey*. The new, sleeker container is tall and rounded, much like a bottle used to carry high-end scotch.

Although he sells Hell Hound white whiskey, O'Hara says the darker, richer spirit is worthy of promotion. He describes it as a combination of scotch and bourbon, melding the grander characteristics of each.

"We got the ten-second burn on the back of the tongue, kind of like a scotch, where the bourbon is usually more front of the tongue. We've kind of got it where the oak and the vanilla hit the front of the tongue hard. There's no char flavor. The back kind of tingles like a scotch, but there's no smokiness, so it seems to make both people happy."

O'Hara worked as an oral prosthetic technician when he was in the navy and now uses those skills in making crowns, bridges, and dentures for his wife, who runs a dental practice in Jacksonville. He started on the distillery in 2012. The idea came from a seemingly benign observation several years earlier. O'Hara, an avid home brewer, makes exotic and unique beers such as Belgian reds and farmhouse ales, which, he says, "taste like wet blankets." Sometime around 2006, when President George W. Bush was pushing ethanol for gasoline and incentivizing its production, O'Hara thought he might give that a go. But he found the profit margin too miniscule. Years later, a friend bragged on O'Hara's beer. O'Hara considered starting a brewery—he hasn't given up on the idea—but it simply cost too much. But a distillery—well, O'Hara thought he could do that.

His first pallets left the farmhouse distillery in 2014.

The distillery was on track to see its first profits in the summer of 2016. Ten percent of that would go toward helping wounded veterans. O'Hara served in Desert Shield and Desert Storm. He remembers the sailors and marines, the airmen and soldiers, many still teenagers. He remembers those who were disfigured, maimed, or killed.

"That always stuck with me. I thought, *If I start making money on liquor, maybe I can help out those guys.*"

O'Hara wanted to call his whiskey Devil Dog, but someone had claimed the trademark.

Phillip O'Hara makes his corn whiskey with yellow corn he grinds at the distillery. It comes from a farm in neighboring Carteret County.
Photo by Lisa Snedeker

Diablo Distilleries   187

"I had a marine colonel who was retired call me, and he said, 'Phil, I heard you're really mad about the Devil Dog thing.' He says, 'Trust me, whenever I yell at a marine, it's, like, "Hey, Devil Dog, get your ass over here."' He said, 'When they go buy a bottle of whiskey, the last thing they want to see is Devil Dog on it. Change it to Hell Hound.'"

Back in World War I, well-armed German soldiers decimated armies across Europe. As O'Hara tells the story, Germans had enveloped a group of U.S. Marines, who refused to surrender. The marines rose up and slaughtered the Germans, save for a few. The marines fought like *teufel hunden*—or, loosely translated, hounds from hell, which eventually morphed into Devil Dogs.

"Hell Hound is really true to history," O'Hara says. "And Devil is probably not what's best for whiskey bottles. I thought, *Well, maybe that was a godsend. We'll change it to Hell Hound.*"

O'Hara, originally from Jellico, Tennessee—a coal town near the Kentucky border—is a one-man show. No partners or investors. He's responsible for sales. In the summer of 2016, he managed to stock Diablo products in eighty of the state's hundred counties.

"I've decided I'm just going to try to cover up the state, make a profit here. That's the thing. Some people don't make a profit here, so they just go to the next state, and they sell two or three pallets, get several grand, go to the next state, get several grand. But the question is, is somebody going to buy the second bottle, the third bottle, or the fifth bottle?"

Near the door of the distillery is a table, its surface covered with mini Mason jars. All are filled with golden brown whiskey. They're unlabeled. He'll get to it.

O'Hara has plans for a tasting room, promotional fliers, T-shirts, and other merchandise. He wants to enhance his website and focus on social media and other marketing means.

All in good time. For now, the whiskey is the thing.

"There's so many ways to blow smoke up people's tails and try to sell whiskey," he says. "I just want to make really good whiskey."

Scotts Point Distillery

Bath, NC
scottspointdistillery.com
The distillery doesn't currently offer tours.

SCOTTS POINT DISTILLERY IN TINY BATH got its license to distill liquor in 2013 and loaded its first pallets for Raleigh in the fall of 2016.

The foundation for the small distillery, its owners say, was the idea that producing quality spirits takes time.

Details matter.

"We've been perfecting our process and letting stuff age and getting our flavors to taste just right, to where we like it," says Toni Jenner, who, along with her husband, Rob, owns the distillery. "We're just a very small craft distillery, and we're taking our time doing it to make sure we put out a quality product."

Scotts Point, the first legal distillery in Beaufort County since Prohibition, makes Pamlico Rum. It uses a light, sweet distiller's molasses sourced in the United States and ages the liquor from six months to two years in Kentucky bourbon barrels. The bottles and labels are made in America, too. So is the pot still, crafted in Maine.

"We believe in supporting quality businesses as close to home as possible," Toni says.

This part of North Carolina, and especially Bath, is pirate country. Edward Teach, a.k.a. Blackbeard, lived off Bath Creek, which leads to the Pamlico River and then to Pamlico Sound.

"All the politicians went to Washington, and all the pirates stayed in Bath," she says.

It's rum country.

Toni says her husband was given a bottle of rum that he found exceptional.

Scotts Point, the first legal distillery in Beaufort County since Prohibition, makes Pamlico Rum.
Photo courtesy of Scotts Point Distillery

He could never find another bottle of that brand, however. That experience, as well as influences from the Caribbean, played no small part in the couple's desire to produce a splendid rum of their own.

Enjoy Pamlico Rum neat or mix it into a Dark 'N' Stormy, Toni suggests.

"Right now, we're really, really small. We're basically trying to figure it out as we go along. Everybody in the industry has been really helpful and open," she says, including the guys from Outer Banks Distilling, located up the coast in Manteo. "When the ABC board didn't have the answer, they did. They were really good guys to talk to."

The distillers have put aside a couple of barrels filled with early, trial batches. Toni says they'll give the golden liquid time to age.

"We're just going to let that go awhile and see what it tastes like in another fifteen years or so. It should be real good by then."

A Think-Tank Report on Alcohol Freedom

North Carolina distillers and people who enjoy locally produced spirits have company in their quest to loosen ABC regulations.

The John Locke Foundation of Raleigh, which promotes free markets and personal freedoms and has a statewide reach, published a study—what it calls a "Spotlight" report—focusing on the maze of rules that hinder entrepreneurship and inhibit expansion of the state's beverage industry.

The report, titled "Hard to Swallow" and authored by Jon Guze, the foundation's director of legal studies, says North Carolina requires forty-three different types of permits and licenses for different activities linked to alcohol sales.

"A new permit is required for every change of ownership of premises licensed to sell alcohol," Guze said in a news release announcing the study. "A rule forbids the owner of multiple premises from moving alcoholic beverages from one location to another. There is a rule restricting happy hours and forbidding some kinds of drink specials, while another forbids distilleries that offer tours from selling any specific visitor more than one bottle of alcohol per year. Rules govern the size of alcoholic beverages in hotel mini-bars and the number of bottles or cans of beer in a case. The list goes on and on.

"For small-time entrepreneurs who want to enter the market for the first time, however, the regulatory regime constitutes a huge barrier. It's very difficult for them to become familiar with the entire body of laws and rules, let alone acquire the expertise and contacts that are needed to deal effectively with all of the relevant agencies."

Guze's report explains how regulations have held back the state in national freedom rankings. North Carolina's overall ranking has jumped from number twenty-six to number nineteen since 2010 in the "Freedom in the 50 States" report compiled by the libertarian Cato Institute. The state, however, lags at number thirty-five in the "Alcohol Freedom" category.

"If we truly want North Carolina to be 'first in freedom,' we need to reduce the burden that excessive regulation places on the production, distribution, and sale of alcoholic beverages," said Guze, who emphasized the state's monopoly on liquor sales, as well as rules governing wholesale distribution of beer and wine.

"The chapter of the N.C. General Statutes dealing specifically with regulation of alcoholic beverages consists of 123 densely packed pages, and many other alcoholic beverage regulations are buried in other parts of the statute book," Guze said. "Chapters of the N.C. Administrative Code dealing with alcohol law enforcement and the Alcoholic Beverage Control Commission take up 143 pages. Again, there are other alcoholic beverage regulations buried in other chapters of the Code."

He called state government's monopoly on liquor sales the "most extreme" alcoholic beverage regulation. "If it weren't for this state monopoly, entrepreneurs would be operating hundreds of private liquor stores in North Carolina, and they would be competing for business with each other and with entrepreneurs operating thousands of grocery stores and other retail outlets. As it is, a limited number of ABC stores keep the same limited hours and charge the same artificially high prices for the same limited selection of products."

The system, he explained, offers a great example of a "bootleggers and Baptists" scenario. "Economists came up with that term to describe a situation in which the Baptists—in this case, concerned citizens—support regulations because they believe those regulations will minimize harms associated with alcohol abuse, while bootleggers—in this case, wholesale distributors and large brewers and distillers—continue to support regulations that protect their jobs, their investments, their power, and their profits."

But there's hope for reform, Guze added. "A new generation of sophisticated consumers is demanding more variety and more quality when it comes to alcoholic beverages, and a new generation of entrepreneurs has emerged to serve them. The entrepreneurs are well aware that the existing regulatory regime protects the big companies at their expense, and they are starting to push back politically. Many consumers are becoming aware as well. There appears to be an emerging coalition of consumers and entrepreneurs ready and able to oppose the long-standing alliance of established interests opposing alcohol freedom."

Outer Banks Distilling

510 Budleigh Street
Manteo, NC 27954
outerbanksdistilling.com
252-423-3011
Distillery tours are offered at 1 P.M. and
3 P.M. Tuesday through Saturday.
Call the distillery from 9 A.M. to 5 P.M.
Tuesday through Saturday to reserve
a spot.

THE OUTER BANKS BEGIN IN SOUTHERN VIRGINIA and skirt the coast of North Carolina. Hurricanes and tropical storms have defined these barrier islands and peninsulas, have rearranged and divided them.

The Outer Banks are rich in history and legend, including stories of Virginia Dare and the Lost Colony. This is where—in part because of the breezes and soft, sandy ground—Wilbur and Orville Wright took off on the first flights in a powered heavier-than-air flying machine. Where Edward Teach, a.k.a. Blackbeard, died, and where his ship, the *Queen Anne's Revenge*, sank, joining a thousand other ill-fated vessels in the aptly named Graveyard of the Atlantic.

Ships carrying spices, sugar, cocoa, and tobacco.

Ships carrying rum.

The rum, which some called "Kill Devil," would wash ashore in barrels, probably from vessels headed for Virginia and New England. The fortunate souls who recovered the barrels hid them among the dunes.

Scott Smith, a native of the Outer Banks, knows the stories. In a way, they are the foundation on which he and three friends built Outer Banks Distilling in Manteo on Roanoke Island.

The friends—Adam Ball, Matt Newsome, and Kelly Bray—have worked in bars and breweries, learning the art of making craft beer and, now, craft rum.

Just rum.

"The brewing industry is so saturated," Smith says. "We could have been followers in the brewing industry, or we could have been leaders in the distilling industry."

They considered making a rye whiskey but ultimately decided against it. It would have been an ode to nearby Buffalo City, a once-thriving timber town that fell on hard times and turned to moonshine, made from notoriously fickle, yet fantastic, rye.

"Maybe if we were two hundred miles inland it would make more sense," Smith says. "Rum is the bread and butter of the Outer Banks. Wherever you have people who like to sail, fish, or surf, everybody likes to drink rum."

Outer Banks Distilling offers two tours each day Tuesday through Saturday. People by the carload—primarily tourists from the Northeast—assemble along Budleigh Street en route to the distillery. It's sort of an OBX Mardi Gras.

"We have a tremendous amount of foot traffic through here," Smith says, "just because of our location and our back story. I think it draws a lot of people in here."

Outer Banks Distilling produces about three thousand cases a year, but a planned expansion could increase output tenfold.
Photo by Lisa Snedeker

The guys started talking about the distillery in 2013 and formed the company in March of that year. They wrote up a business plan, gathered the necessary money, and pitched their idea to the townspeople.

"Land is very valuable on the Outer Banks. There's not so much of it," Smith says. "We came over here and we saw there are a lot of buildings that needed some restoration."

The townspeople welcomed the idea, confident in the friends and eager to tout their small but stunningly beautiful community.

"We weren't going to be cutting any corners, we weren't going to be having it made."

Smith is referring to grain-neutral spirits, much of which are made in the Midwest.

"We weren't trying to just sell the name. We actually wanted to make it here. The Outer Banks is a very tight-knit community. It wasn't like we were talking to people we had never met before. We were dealing with people we've known for a long time. Then we started talking about how we wanted to renovate this building, and that went a long way with people, too."

They bought the building in January 2014. Built in 1946 as a furniture store by the family that now operates the funeral home next door, it later became a department store and was home to the Dare County Board of Education. The board left it in 2003. The building had been cut up into offices and portioned by cubicles—part of what became twenty tons of scrap.

"It took us a whole year to renovate it, because we ended up cutting everything out of here," Smith says.

They cut through the floor to pour ten inches of concrete and removed a massive part of the ceiling to accommodate the column still.

Larry Bray, a local builder, woodcrafter, and artist—and Kelly Bray's father—oversaw and encouraged much of the work.

"He's the one who came in here and really convinced us we could do the building by ourselves," Smith says. "He came over here and gave us the time and expertise to make this building really have this character, so we've got to give him the credit."

Save the wood, he told them—the locally harvested cypress from the floor joists and the heart-pine floor. What came out was returned to use, repurposed and renewed. The front door and counter are from the original cypress, as are picture frames and carvings made by Larry Bray. The tasting bar and trim are from the heart pine.

The distillery hosted a ceremonial ribbon cutting in February 2015.

Outer Banks Distilling in Manteo bottles its unique Kill Devil Rum infused with pecans and honey.
Photo by Lisa Snedeker

It was to be a little event. The guys expected maybe 50 people. Some 350 showed up.

They asked where the rum was.

"Actually," Smith remembers telling them, "we have to start making it now."

Each batch consists of about 720 bottles. The first such run—sixty cases—sold out in four hours.

The distillery's unaged silver Kill Devil Rum is made from Louisiana molasses, which brings a subtle sweetness that transfers to the glass—"Molasses to glasses," in fact, is the distillery's trademark mantra.

"You'll get that sweetness of the molasses up front, and you'll notice it's got a lot of earth tones," Smith says. "You taste a lot of the almond, a little bit of citrus, and then on the back end I get toasted marshmallow and some licorice. It's got a nice, clean finish to it. There's not a lot of edges on it."

The molasses is stored in thousand-gallon totes, which are emptied in about a week.

The distillery produces about three thousand cases a year, but a planned expansion could increase output tenfold. Smith says the guys are maxing things out. Their plans call for a still three times as large as the present one.

Outer Banks Distilling also produces a delightful concoction that smells of candied nuts. Made with pecans and honey—from Manns Harbor and

Wanchese, respectively—this rum is an ode to grandmas, family holidays, and all things wholesome and good. "I don't think anybody was going to buy shrimp or flounder or oyster rum, so we decided to take it in a different direction," Smith says.

The distillery parrots the style and character of rums made in Martinique and Guadeloupe in the French West Indies, even advancing French artistry and techniques. "They really like to harvest the flavor of the raw ingredient, bring it out in each bottle," Smith says. "That's one of our goals. We get a lot of earth tones to it, a lot of real body and texture. A lot of rums are really light and grassy, and that's not what our real goal is."

Outer Banks has a three-hundred-liter Holstein copper still and a nine-plate rectifying column, which visitors can see through the large windows separating the tasting room and gift shop from the distillery.

"It really is made right here. That's us making it," Smith says. "It really goes a long way with some people who don't necessarily have the time to take the tour."

The distilling days are long and arduous, yet Smith insists the owners won't relinquish control of their public tours. It's an important part of the experience, he says. "I really don't want to pay someone else to do the tours. It's still our baby. Right now, we're just four guys trying to do everything hands-on, and I think people appreciate that when they come and see. Matt and I trade off doing the tours. We consider ourselves kind of the front-of-the-house guys. Kelly and Adam are more of the back-of-the-house guys."

On a far wall of the distillery, rum ages in barrels that once held bourbon for Jim Beam. A three-year rum is planned for release in 2018. The distillery is also working on a "Shipwreck" series and a Blackbeard's Reserve, to debut on the three hundredth anniversary of his death, which, according to lore, happened in a blaze of gunfire on November 22, 1718.

It's a summer Monday under a pristine Carolina blue sky. It's morning, but the temperature is rising with the sun. Budleigh Street is weirdly quiet, preternaturally empty. Shallowbag Bay is a few blocks east, but you can feel the ocean in the air and almost taste the salt water. A tepid breeze reveals a note of wild honeysuckle—and of molasses that's becoming rum.

The tranquility will dissipate when tours begin Tuesday. The happy chaos continues for most of the calendar year but tapers off in November, when tourists leave and an ocean chill sets in.

Then it's time to work, says Smith. "We use the extra time to keep our heads down and crank out as much rum as possible."

Index

Index   199